"Sieglinde Othmer stands as a beacon of hope and inspiration . . . she is a testament to the fact that life's most exquisite adventures often await us in the later chapters and that the pursuit of well-being is a journey worth embarking upon, at any age."

—**Dr. David Friedman,** International Award-Winning, #1 Best-Selling Author of *Food Sanity,* Syndicated TV/Radio Host, Keynote Speaker

"It's no wonder that Sieglinde Othmer has a smile with such warmth. *Joyous Longevity* reveals the secret to her vibrancy. And I want some of that! I love the stories she shares to which we can all relate. *Joyous Longevity* is not only for people of a certain age, but it is also for people wishing to reach that certain age having maintained a great quality of life. *Joyous Longevity* is a life enhancing tool. Enjoy this guide. I certainly did and will share it with others. It offers steps that, if followed, fortify your ability to remain independent and to thrive."

—**Silver Wainhouse,** Joy Artisan, Certified Coach, Founder/Director of the Black Joy Lab

"A quick and delightful read."

—**Annette Barrie,** Avon Representative for Fifty Years

"*Joyous Longevity* is a terrific combination of storytelling and education on living one's best life. The author takes readers on a journey through her life experiences traveling the globe and pursuing new ventures. She has a zest for life that is obvious and pervasive throughout her book. Her concepts are both simple and inspiring. The reader gets the opportunity to live vicariously through the author's adventures while accumulating ideas to improve habits that create a better life for themselves. *Joyous Longevity* is a quick, energetic, and informative read that will help many readers live life to its fullest by pursuing their dreams in both big and small ways."

—**Chris Carr,** Awesome Friend and Family Man

"Winston Churchill said, 'A diplomat is a person who can tell you to go to hell in such a way that you would actually look forward to the trip.' This quote came to mind when reading this delightful book. Instead of dreading getting old, Sieglinde's wonderful A to Z approach to aging provides us fellow travelers with inspirational, motivating, fun and creative ideas to maximize every moment of our gift of life."

—**Joan Israelite,** Consultant at Kauffman Center for the Performing Arts, Kansas City

"This book, like the YMCA, stands as a beacon, promoting a positive perspective on aging and championing the belief that each passing year is a testament to resilience, wisdom, and a life well-lived. With Sieglinde's field guide, I look forward to the journey into the later years with a twinkle in my eye and unfinished tasks ahead."

—**Mark Hulet,** President and CEO, YMCA of Greater Kansas City

"A delightful and inspiring read for people of all ages. Sieglinde Othmer is a wise woman with a whimsical and inviting writing style. In *Joyous Longevity,* she offers delicious tidbits for creating a more vibrant, fun, and meaningful life. Interspersed are her own fascinating stories, those of a woman who has explored both the world and herself. Enrich your life by treating yourself and a friend to this book."

—**Deborah Shouse,** Author, *An Old Woman Walks Into a Bar*

"Sieglinde Othmer has collected an essential primer, a series of simple pathways through the complex courses that pepper our lives. These truths will excite and inspire you to maximize our most finite resource— time. She underscores a fundamental fact: when in doubt, step on the gas."

—**Dan Navarro**, Singer, Songwriter, Voice Actor

"In a world where the relentless march of time can bring with it iso- lation and a diminished sense of purpose, this manuscript emerges as a beacon of hope and a testament to the unconquerable spirit of those who have journeyed through decades of life's challenges. It is a masterful symphony of wisdom, a celebration of life lived with zest, and an unwavering commitment to personal growth and fulfillment.

Crafted with the precision of a seasoned scholar and the warmth of a lifelong friend, this work invites us into the intimate reflections of a life lived through the lens of abundance, from the wanderlust-driven explorations of youth through the complex tapestries of love, loss, and the quest for meaning in the later chapters of life. It is a sentinel call to rediscover the joys of independence, creativity, and connection, even in the face of adversity's stark image.

With elegance and empathy, the author weaves together personal anecdotes with universal truths, guiding us through the seasons of life with the gentle hand of someone who has navigated its tumultuous waters and emerged with insights both luminous and life-affirming. This manuscript is not merely a collection of reflections but a vibrant mosaic of strategies for thriving in the autumn of one's years, a toolkit for those brave souls who dare to approach aging not as a decline but as a new horizon ripe with possibility.

In endorsing this manuscript, I do so with the conviction that its pages hold the power to transform the way we perceive aging, independence, and joy. It stands as a tribute to the resilience of the human spirit, a guidepost for those seeking to infuse their later years with the richness and vibrancy that life, in all its complexity, has to offer. Let us embark on this journey with open hearts and minds, ready to embrace the art of living with the same courage and curiosity that has guided its author through the decades. Herein lies not just a manual for aging gracefully but a manifesto for living deeply, passionately, and unapologetically at any age."

—**Patrick H. Tyrance, Jr., MD**, Founder/Owner
TyranceOrthopedics.com and AvastarCryo.com

JOYOUS
LONGEVITY

JOYOUS LONGEVITY

THE A-Z FIELD GUIDE

SIEGLINDE OTHMER

Illustrations by Julia C. Othmer

Foreword by Dr. David Friedman

Published by Joyous Longevity Books, LLC, Kansas City, MO

ISBN (paperback): 978-1-7376028-0-4
ISBN (ebook): 978-1-7376028-1-1
ISBN (audio book): 978-1-7376028-2-8

Book design and production by www.AuthorSuccess.com

Printed in the United States of America

Disclaimer
The author has made every effort to assure the accuracy of the information presented. The author disclaims any liability whatsoever with respect to any loss, injury, or damage resulting from reading this book. The author is not a licensed dietician, health care professional, personal trainer, psychologist, or psychotherapist. She draws her knowledge from research and from her professional and personal experience. She is sharing what she has learned in eighty years of life. This book is not intended as a substitute for consulting with your physician or other healthcare provider. It is intended to provide helpful and informative material on the subjects presented in this publication.

Contents

"If you don't like something, change it.
If you can't change it, change your attitude."
~ Maya Angelou ~

Foreword

by Dr. David Friedman

Joyous Longevity: The A-Z Field Guide is an extraordinary journey through the tapestry of life, brilliantly woven by Sieglinde Othmer. As I delve into these pages, I am reminded of the age-old saying that "age is but a number." Sieglinde, at eighty-two years young, is a testament to the power of the human spirit, resilience, and the unwavering pursuit of happiness, regardless of the challenges life may throw our way.

Her story begins with a stark and relatable moment—a morning that marked the beginning of a new chapter in her life. She awoke at the ripe age of eighty with her beloved husband no longer by her side, her children living far away, and the profound question echoing in her heart: "What now?" It's a moment that many of us, at some point in our lives, will confront—an intersection of solitude and reflection.

But Sieglinde, in her wisdom and fortitude, refused to let this juncture define her. She cast her gaze back to her spirited youth, where she was a trailblazer, an explorer, and a seeker of experiences. With a determined spirit, she sought to recapture the essence of her younger self. The challenges of life had sculpted her, but they did not define her. Then, as fate would have it, the world was gripped by the COVID-19 pandemic. Isolation and uncertainty descended upon us all. Sieglinde, with her ever-present ability to find the silver lining, embraced this time to rediscover her love for music, particularly opera. It was through this art form that she found solace and joy, and her spirit soared.

With spring's return, her garden blossomed, and so did she. The renewed sense of happiness and curiosity led her to embark on a remarkable journey of self-discovery, culminating in the creation of this extraordinary guide. In *Joyous Longevity*, Sieglinde shares twenty-six practical ideas, each representing a letter of the alphabet, to guide readers on a path of gratitude and joyous longevity. It's her way of extending a hand to those who may be in their sixties, seventies, or even eighty-five-plus, reassuring them that life's adventure is far from over.

Sieglinde stands as a beacon of hope and inspiration, reporting from the front lines of a life that has spanned continents, careers, and experiences. Her journey has been one of ups and downs, from refugee to world traveler, academic to businessperson, wife, and mother. She has borne witness to suffering and healing, and she knows the impact of both medical interventions and simple changes in habits. In other words, Sieglinde Othmer has indeed "been around the block."

As you embark on this incredible journey through each page, do so with an open heart, a curious spirit, and a willingness to embrace the wisdom of an author who has truly lived and continues to live the life she advocates for. Sieglinde is a testament to the fact that life's most exquisite adventures often await us in the later chapters and that the pursuit of well-being is a journey worth embarking upon, at any age.

Dr. David Friedman
International Award-Winning,
#1 Best-Selling Author of *Food Sanity*
Syndicated TV/Radio Host
Keynote Speaker

Winding Up

One morning I woke up and suddenly I was eighty. Holy moly. How in the world did that happen? And to boot, my husband of fifty-five years had just died. My kids lived far away. Alone with myself, I wondered what now?

I remembered a feeling from my youth—being on my own and loving it. Nineteen and chestnut-haired, I was studying at the university in Hamburg, Germany, and at the Sorbonne in Paris. During semester breaks, I explored Belgium, France, and Spain by train, bundled in my moss-green corduroy coat. Thrifty by nature and necessity, I spent each night in hostels and convents, where nuns shared their bread and milk for supper. My curiosity led me to delve into colorful cultures, learning their languages and dances. I embraced my independence with gusto.

Marriage certainly changed my priorities. Immigration to the United States happened. Three kids, three dogs, a career in academia, then business career. Family life demanded my attention 24/7. There was love, lots of effort, and more love.

Now, staring at my future at eighty, it all seemed as dry as the Mojave Desert. How could I capture that feeling of being on my own and loving it as I did at nineteen? How could I recover the feeling of being independent and thriving?

Then, Covid hit. Isolation. I went gray. Silver gray.

To cheer me up, I used to write. So, I created a story of seven cousins—five dogs and two cats—who, tired of being only pets, decided to undertake an adventure. They became entertainers who traveled and wowed the world with their performances. But that lost its luster during Covid.

I like to laugh and seek things that bring me merriment so as not to succumb to dreariness. Great music, especially musical comedy, lightened me. During that trying Covid time, every night at 6:30, the Metropolitan Opera in New York offered free telecasts as their way to connect and support the public. So, every night, I watched operas, the finest productions ever, brilliantly presented on my computer. There was a different one every twenty-four hours. Their beauty transported me away from gloom. I had always loved Beethoven, Mozart, and Rossini, but now I discovered Richard Wagner. I never knew that Giuseppe Verdi wrote *Falstaff* at eighty. At the age of eighty! That was an inspiration for me. Art got me through the first Covid winter.

When spring returned, my garden woke up, and so did I. Even though the pandemic continued, I felt renewed happiness and wanted to explore more of life. But opera every night? Out of the question, especially since I was looking forward to another thirty years. I needed other things to do with my evenings. I wanted to find ways to develop and maintain habits that brought and maintained the joy I was feeling. My explorations launched this book.

I collected twenty-six practical ideas, short bites, and suggestions for joyous longevity, for myself and for you, my dear reader. You may be sixty, seventy, or older. This book is about the ABCs of aging intentionally with wisdom, grace, and fun.

This A-Z field guide will:

* ❋   Change the way you think about aging

* ❋   Motivate you to adopt habits that support healthy longevity

* ❋   Inspire you to be more active

* ❋   Get your butt out of the house and keep you moving

* ❋   Enrich your day-to-day enjoyment of life

I have had the good fortune of living and working with diverse groups of people and learning from them. It is one of the treasures for which I am grateful to have received in life. I've been poor, I've been rich, an academic, a businessperson, a wife, and a mother. As a World War II refugee, I lived through post-war Germany and France. I traveled deeply into Europe, then to Africa, Asia, Australia, and the Americas. As a research assistant in the Department of Psychiatry at Washington University in St. Louis, Missouri, as manager of sleep labs at the University of Kentucky and the University of Kansas Medical Center, and as an investigator in drug research and administrator of our psychiatric clinic, I have witnessed first-hand stress and suffering. Observing that suffering was helped by medical interventions and by changes in habits, I took note. I've been around the block.

At my annual check-up, I asked my family physician, who himself happens to be over eighty, "What's most important at eighty?"

He chuckled, "Stay on this side of the grass."

On the way home, a voice inside me giggled and whispered, *this can be way more than just surviving. This is about kicking ass.*

If you've never kicked ass, and we all have wanted to, what are you waiting for? There are five million members of the octogenarian club in the USA alone, and a gazillion more across the globe. We have outlived, outlasted, and laughed at the statistics of the expected 4,001 weeks of human life. We have our own math table, and we are not winding down. No! We're winding up, and it's because we rejoice at the great fortune to be alive. Scientists are talking about the possibility of living to be 120 with advances in medicine and a reasonably healthy lifestyle. That means that eighty is a mere portal to longevity. We have a pretty good chance to live to a really old, mega Methuselah age. Alleluia.

Hey! Aging is natural, neutral, and non-negotiable. It happens to everyone, no matter what. We cannot control it, but we *can* control how we handle it. We *can* control how we think about it. I encourage you to start by thinking about age as a privilege, a badge of honor, by taking pride in it and not being ashamed of your aging body. You are defined by your attitudes and actions. It *is* possible to have a bigger share of the good that life offers—adventure, excitement, joy—and minimize the impact of the not-so-good-betrayal, illness, and loss. I propose we take the path of curiosity and lightness.

Let's cultivate what the French call *L'Art de Vivre,* the Art of Living. It's about delighting in life's small things, like really appreciating that first cup of coffee in the morning and being blanketed with the aroma. Enjoy yourself in animated conversation with friends by being totally present. Take outdoor walks. Spot crocuses peeking through the snow. Let the smell of lavender calm you. Eat your dinner not in the car or in front of the television or computer screen, but at a table with a flower as the centerpiece. Search for simplicity and you will find pleasure that comes every day and stays.

As we start our journey together, I'm in my eighties. I'm bringing you magic with the magical number eighty. The eight when lying on its belly symbolizes infinity. It signifies eternity, which we all face, sooner or later. In Chinese culture, eight means abundance, harmony, and success. It embodies the balance between the material and the spiritual way of existence. Zero, in many traditions, means the circle of life. So, eighty opens immense possibilities and brings good fortune.

That being the case, roll up your sleeves and put on your dancing shoes and whatever music gets you moving. We are beginning.

CHAPTER 1

A for AWAKE

Gratitude, the Best Starter

*"Just one small positive thought in the
morning can change your whole day."*
~ The Dalai Lama ~

The first thing that happens to us upon awakening is body awareness. Every fiber of our being registers, I'm alive and alert. Ah! Each day we wake up is (at least somewhat) a good day. Yes?

Before getting out of bed, I follow a routine to ease into complete wakefulness. This is *My Morning Ritual (MMR)*. To be sure to get my day off to the right start, I consciously choose to take this special time for myself.

While warm and cozy under the covers, I put my brain to work. I revive it by orienting myself. I ask myself what day it is. What did I have for dinner last night? Did I watch a movie? I note the time.

Then, my attention turns to my physical body. I stimulate it with movement. While still in bed, I rotate my feet. To the left and to the right—they will carry me all day. I twist. I wiggle my fingers. I squirm, raise my hips gently, pull my knees to my chin. I stretch my body as far as I can. I make a snow angel. Intentionally, I make my lips form a smile, knowing that my brain will register this and boost my mood. I drink some water from the glass I keep by my bed. No rush. Easy going.

To brush away any cobwebs of anxiety, I embrace gratitude. I name three things I'm grateful for. I'm giving thanks for my body that kept me alive through the night. The body is a miraculous thing. I acknowledge the sleep I got, whatever quality and length it was. I initiate the feeling of gratitude for the roof over my head. You may surprise yourself with *your own list of things to be thankful for*. Filling the heart with positivity sets the attitude for the morning.

Then I sit up. I grab a pen and paper from my nightstand and write down the part of any dream I can remember or the solution to a problem I wrestled with yesterday and that my sleeping mind solved for me. I do this before I forget. I keep a morning journal, noting whatever comes to mind; like a check-in with my soul. Only then do I get out of bed.

Once in the kitchen, I turn on the radio, make coffee, drink a large glass of water, and take my tonic: a tablespoon of elderberry syrup. I go outside, feel the temperature, fetch the paper, and look at the sky. Sunrises can be breathtaking. Back inside with my coffee cup, I read the paper. I locate my mobile and look for messages from family and friends. I practice French with the Duolingo app for fifteen minutes. To wake up my speaking voice for the day, I say the French phrases out loud. I get dressed to go outside for the second time of the morning to check in with my flowers at the front door. I feed my birds and I take a walk. By doing this routine, I have found that a good day has begun.

A ritual does not have to be a rut. *MMR* sometimes gets adjusted. Early morning appointments or projects, like writing this book, cause me to get up at 5:00 a.m. The world is quiet until the sun comes up. I know when it's 7:00 because that's when my neighbor across the street starts his truck. His *MMR*.

Action steps for AWAKE:

Jot down your first few thoughts of the day.

Plant an affirmation that invigorates you and makes you want to get up.

What is your morning routine?
Email me about it at joyouslongevity@gmail.com

CHAPTER 2

B for BELIEVING

Believe It and You Will Be It

"Whether you think you can, or you can't, you're right."
~ Henry Ford ~

What you believe determines your well-being. Your belief influences how you feel about yourself and others. Your belief is like a filter that colors how you see the world. You choose what you believe. What you believe is your reality.

First and foremost, believe in yourself. If you have accepted beliefs that have dimmed your candle, it's time to let go of those beliefs. Feed your flame so it glows brightly. Like Eleanor Roosevelt stated, "No one can make you feel inferior without your consent." You do not have to fade as you get older. You can rally. This is YOUR time.

Believe in the healing power of your own body. Western medicine doctors call it the *placebo effect.* It's the strong belief that a treatment will help, even though the pill may have no active ingredients, or the procedure may be non-specific, even in surgery. Belief activates the body's self-healing capabilities in a most powerful way. You gotta believe your body wants to heal.

Believe in people's goodness (until proven otherwise). Believe in possibilities. Believe in everything that brings greater joy and kindness into your life. Visualize positive outcomes. Believe your team will win.

Believe that life will work out for you, that brain and body will stay together, parallel, to the end. Three times a day say out loud: "I'm happy, healthy, and very good-looking."

I believe in supernatural phenomena and in guardian angels. I recognize their presence in my life when I notice angel numbers. 11:11, 3:33, 5:55. Why not stop for a moment and make a wish? 'Angel' comes from the Greek word *angelos*, meaning messenger or spirit guide. I believe there are guides who we can call upon. Believe in your sense of deep knowing. Believe in your intuition. Believe your gut. Believe in synchronicity, in meaningful coincidences. Believe in magic. What have you got to lose?

I was driving in a downtown construction zone. About to change lanes, I heard this voice in my head saying "*NO!*" Just then, a motorcyclist roared past, only inches from a collision. Where did that *no* come from? Was that my spirit guide protecting me? Prospero in Shakespeare's *Tempest* claims, "we are all spirits."

In the dark years of World War II, my father, drafted at age forty-two, was fighting in Russia. My mother went to see a psychic, looking for guidance. That psychic told her that she would move far away. To the water. My mother dismissed that as strange. She would never leave Meissen, the land-locked town in Saxony, Germany, the town she loved. During peacetime, my father was a teacher there and a theater critic. Together, they enjoyed the latest shows from front-row seats. But my mother kept the psychic's words in her heart. After the war, she smuggled herself and me across the East-West German border to reunite with my father. She built a new life in Hamburg. Hamburg is located on the Elbe River between the North Sea and the Baltic Sea. Just a little bit of water. How did that psychic know? There are parallel universes.

I believe that we hold memories of past lives. Some of us, on occasion, experience feelings of familiarity, predisposition, preference, yearning, a pull to a certain geographical area—we all have different degrees of sensibility. When I was nineteen, on a trip to Bruges, Belgium, after a walk through town I sat on a stone bench on a low bridge crossing one of the canals. Looking at the picturesque fifteenth-century houses, there came a strong feeling of comfort over me, as though *I had been here before.* The sensation of belonging was like a cultural grounding. How far back do our memories go?

A year later, I visited the medieval fortress of Carcassonne in Southern France and stood on its ramparts. Alone. There it was again, this sense of knowing that *I had been here before.* Enthralled with the place, I used all thirty-six precious exposures on the film in my Leica to capture everything—the castle walls, the parapets, the spiral staircases, the turrets, and the arrow loops that opened to vistas of the countryside. Eager to take more pictures, but not knowing my camera enough (there was no photo shop anywhere to help me), I put in a new roll, ruining the exposed film and the new one by exposing both to light. Sixty years later, I visited the same place. Carcassonne had changed into a crowded tourist attraction, but I had the same feeling of intimacy. On top of that, I realized that the human rights activist and hero of my doctoral dissertation, Jean Barbeyrac, a French Huguenot, the fellow I spent years researching way back when, he was born in that region of France in 1674. Go figure that connection.

I have a third story. As an au pair student in Paris, every day from 1:00 to 8:00 p.m., I took care of two little boys. In my free time, I studied at the Sorbonne and socialized with my peers, singing in the choir, going to dances, and traveling by train to Versailles. On Tuesdays, the Louvre had no admission fee, so I went once a week. Of the 380,000 art objects on display, one especially stunned me. Not the Mona Lisa; she seemed like an old lady. What drew my attention was the statue of a male scribe, a funerary sculpture made of limestone from Saqqara, Egypt. Dressed in a white kilt he is seated, holding a half-rolled papyrus in his lap, his right hand poised to write. The life-like rock crystal eyes of this 4,500-year-old man mesmerized me. I felt a weird connection; I was only nineteen years old. Then life happened, and I forgot about him.

Forty-five years later, I visited the Louvre again with my husband and my oldest son. The Mona Lisa looked surprisingly young, and I found my scribe. From a framed postcard, he now observes me from my study wall. Maybe he symbolizes what I was supposed to do with my life. As he waited for instructions from his pharaoh, I sat here with my empty page waiting for ideas. Who dictates to me? He's my inspiration.

For your consideration about BELIEVING:

What do you believe to be true about yourself?

What do you believe about your body?

About money?

About luck?

About love?

Have you ever had a nudge experience?

Are you, too, collecting evidence of past lives?

CHAPTER 3

C for CREATIVITY

Magic

"Creativity takes courage."
~ Henri Matisse ~

We all are makers. We are all creators. Our masterpiece of creation is how we live our lives.

Being creative does not necessarily mean reinventing the wheel. It can mean doing *old* things in *new* ways. Like knitting hearts or socks to save them from becoming washrags. Like shoveling snow in a crisscross pattern. Like scouting mom-and-pop nurseries for unusual plants. Last fall, I stuck one hundred crocus bulbs into my lawn for spring's first show of color. The crocus will bloom before the grass ever gets cut.

When my husband and I first came to this country for a government research job on a one-year contract, we took out a loan to pay for our flights from Luxembourg via Reykjavik to New York to Saint Louis. The exchange rate, US dollar to the German mark, was one to four. Parsimony was required. How to save American pennies? With creativity. We decorated an empty rental house with thrift store furniture. Six mismatched chairs and an odd table with legs of turned wood from the 1950s transformed into an unusual fine dining set by painting them all in the same color: brilliant white. I still have one of those chairs, the one we bought for $2.50.

I love writing. After a career of strictly academic output, I needed relief. To change course. To start fresh. To do something different. To rekindle my imagination. To go wild. To have fun. So, I tried fiction writing. And hey! It was glorious. I created a whole new world where real pets from my family—five dogs and two cats—became artists and toured the world with their shows. Illustrations made my characters come alive. Allowing myself to have a creative mindset made my life richer.

Crafting is a big creative thing. Paper. Quilting. Tapestry. Weaving. Wood. You can be creative using your hands or a sewing machine. Have you ever tried making your own holiday cards? Could you create a Halloween haunted house for the neighborhood kids to enjoy? Even bolder would be installing a zipline in your backyard. Paint a room in bold blue. Would you hesitate in front of the empty canvas, paintbrush in hand? No! Have courage! Slap on the color! No self-imposed limits.

My younger son sent me this clay sculpting stuff. I stared at it at first, then got started. I cleared a table, covered it with old newspapers to catch the mess, and sculpted with thin strips and fat rolls of clay, in all the colors the set came with. In my dream world, I always wanted to have chickens, but my county does not allow them in my neighborhood . . . yet. So, from that clay, I made myself a whole flock—four different sized exotic hens and one rooster, with attitudes. They now sit on my windowsill to amuse me. The next generation of chickens will be wearing yellow scarves and purple hats. As soon as it is allowed, I'll get live ones and give them names.

Creativity is a great way to handle a situation and help you out of a pickle. For example, if you ever try line dancing in an *AB* (meaning *Absolute Beginner*) class, and you happen to get out of line, you can make up your own steps and still swing along to the music.

Creativity and experimenting hold hands like lovers. Like in cooking. It can be simple or fancy. Four or fourteen ingredients. I challenge my palate with new spices. Once a week, I try out a new recipe or make up a new one. I surprise myself, like with homemade pink lentil soup or cauliflower curry or cauliflower steaks. If my endeavor doesn't yield gourmet results, so what? I keep doing it. You, too, can be brave.

Making art is how we frolic. If you raise a brow, here is pen and paper. I suggest the haiku, the Japanese freestyle form of poetry that has only three lines. The first line is five syllables, then seven, then five. It could be something like this:

Come together now.
For dancing, joking, playing.
Gladness in the heart.

Pointers for CREATIVITY:

Take one thing down from your walls and hang up *your own* creation. Like a collage, a drawing, a painting, a motto in large letters, or your art piece made from twigs, twine, and a loved object.

Start your memoir. Write ten minutes each day. You'll be amazed how it grows.

Crochet a dragon egg.

Make your own haiku.

And dream up your next creation.

CHAPTER 4

D for DRESS

The Bloom That Won't Wilt

*"The finest clothing is a person's skin, but, of course,
society demands something more than this."*
~ Mark Twain ~

I love to play dress up like a kid, except I do it for real. When I wear something that I love, it feels good. When you feel good, folks respond to your positive energy. Make a conscious decision to present yourself to the world in whatever makes you feel assertive. Go for color. For pizazz. When, if not now?

Dress for dignity. Dress for confidence, prestige, and pride. Dress for your own respect. Theatrical garments with chunky jewelry have set the stage for centuries. Clothes project notability.

Dress for power. Clothes heighten visibility. Be seen! You are not a mouse. You project presence through what you are wearing. Make a style statement. This is the time of your life. How you dress makes a difference. They say to *dress for success* and *to dress to impress.* I say dress for less stress.

Dress for comfort. For pleasure. For softness. It's important. Get rid of clothes that don't fit. Too tight today is also too tight tomorrow. Get rid of items that evoke any kind of bad memory. Wear things you love. Aren't you done worrying about your body shape? I am. Let that worry go. Have fun and more fun. You deserve it. Wear vests, tunics, gloves, hats, and—yes—those striped pants. May I mention the orange scarf, the boutonniere, the multi-hued caftan, and the glittery dinner jacket with red heels? Ease your mind with clothes.

Dress for the occasion. Way back as a fresh immigrant, my husband, the doctor, dressed down when he went to haggle for a used car. He felt that if he looked too well dressed, the car salesman wouldn't give him as good a deal.

The British have a fondness for *Fancy Dress.* It's not what I thought it would be, like an evening gown and black tie. No. The *Fancy Dress* request on a dinner party invitation means that you express yourself that evening, as in *whatever you want to be.* Sometimes there are specific themes, but if that is not noted, go as it suits you. Like showing up as *Happiness* in a pink suit or as a *Gift* wrapped in tissue. Arrive as a Caesar, Cleopatra, a daffodil, a frog prince, or a seahorse. Whatever strikes your fancy. Make the costume from stuff you have lying around (ha!).

You look like an interesting person, someone might say, and your response might be, *aren't we all interesting?* Here begins a memorable evening.

Ideas for DRESS: Embarking on a new fun phase of life.

Make fashion a pleasure.

What fabrics do you like? Bamboo, cotton, fringe, lace, sequins, silk, velvet, or wool?

What colors? Bright, muted, or extravagant?

Dare to embrace a fresh look.

Grow a mustache.

Dress up for dinner.

And, above all, add this important piece of wardrobe: your smile.

CHAPTER 5

E for EATING WELL

You are What You Eat. Really.

"Let food be thy medicine."
~ Hippocrates ~

It's simple. To live long, you must eat well. If you nourish a plant with good soil, proper nutrients, and enough water, it will thrive. If you don't, you know the results. Same with the body. Say it with me now, *to live long we must eat well.*

How do we eat well to live long?

Dan Buettner, an American National Geographic Fellow, searched the planet and found six places where women and men consistently live in good health to the age of one hundred and beyond. He called these areas Blue Zones. They are spread out all over the globe.

❋   California: Loma Linda

❋   Costa Rica: Nicoya

❋   Greece: Icaria

❋   Italy: Sardinia

✳   Japan: Okinawa

✳   Singapore

It turns out that longevity is not due to a special environment and/or the genetics of certain fortunate tribes. Longevity is due to lifestyle. Big time.

Blue Zone people all over the world share nine habits:

✳   Mostly eating plant-based meals

✳   Stopping when 80 percent full

✳   Enjoying moderate wine drinking at 5:00 p.m.

✳   Exercising regularly

✳   Reducing stress

✳   Living with a purpose

✳   Practicing spirituality

✳   Engaging with family

✳   Having reliable friends

Notice that the first three deal with food. The next three are habits under our control (see chapters M for Moving, Q for Quietude, and P for Purpose). The last three deal with the relationships we cultivate with higher powers and with people (see chapters B for Believe and S for Socializing). Relationships can feed us something delicious or starve us and can even be poisonous.

By now, everyone has heard that ultra-processed food is bad, Bad, BAD. It has been endlessly linked to obesity and chronic disease. So! Toss the canned soups! Toss the frozen cardboard boxes! Toss the stuff with cryptic, unpronounceable chemicals and preservatives. You want to eat fresh food. Fresh veggies fill you up sooner and longer. They improve blood pressure, blood sugar levels, cholesterol, digestion, energy, mood, sleep, skin, and weight. How amazing it would be for our bodies if we all ate more plants, not to mention how amazing it would be for our planet. What a giant co-benefit!

As to food habits number two and three, don't overeat. Your stomach will enjoy looking forward to the next meal. If you have a glass of wine, have it at five in the evening! Why at five? By the time you go to bed, your body has processed the alcohol, and your sleep will be better.

Cook! Make your own interesting meals! The act of cooking can create the feeling of happiness and satisfaction. A plate loaded with colorful veggies is known to delight the most ravenous meat eater's appetite. Try roasted carrots, broccoli, and brussels sprouts drizzled with olive oil, red lentil stew, and cucumber salad. Or just an idea, cut two yellow onions and two fennel bulbs into quarters, put them in your favorite baking dish, douse them with a jar of marinated artichokes, add a little olive oil, and pop them into the oven at 400 degrees for thirty minutes. This makes a party favorite.

Courage! For a long time, I thought quiche was the most wonderful flaky yummy treat. The Italians have been at it since the thirteenth century. When the French took it over, they called it Quiche Lorraine. Making it myself? Never dared, because I lived with a man who disliked it, who harmonized with the 1980s book, *Real Men Don't Eat Quiche*. I had a FEAR of being ridiculed over quiche. Over fricking quiche. So silly of me! Now I know FEAR stands for False Evidence Appearing Real. In this new phase of life, I'm going for it, and you can too. To make the dough, all you need is a clean smooth surface, a rolling pin or empty wine bottle, flour, butter, and ice water, and for the filling, you need eggs, cream, cheese, and cooked veggies. Put all of it into an oven-proof dish for forty-five minutes at 350 degrees. Don't worry about the mess in the kitchen. If the crust is a bother, make the quiche crustless. Bake just the filling. That's totally fine, and even healthier because you will be skipping the flour and butter.

Praise be to cabbage, the cheapest superfood there is. Slice it thin, stir it with olive oil and cut up onions, fresh garlic, caraway or cumin seeds, salt, pepper, and ginger if you like. Add a little water and cook on the stove for fifteen minutes or bake it in the oven. You've got yourself a healthy, hearty side dish. If consumed often, cabbage reduces the risk of cancer. Two and a half millennia ago, Hippocrates, the founder of Western medicine, called cabbage "the vegetable of a thousand virtues." Cabbage is a brassica, also called cruciferous veggies, same family as arugula, Bok choy, broccoli, brussels sprouts, cauliflower, chard, kohlrabi, mustard greens, and white, red, and savoy cabbage. They are all loaded with fiber and vitamins, and they go with almost anything. Like The Beatles' Ringo Star stated, "Peace, love, broccoli. I'm ninety-nine percent broccoli."

Eat yourself to better health.

EATING WELL guidelines:

Sport a stylish apron.

Fix a veggie new to you. You, the daredevil cook. Or fix a common veggie in a new way, like carrots with mustard and honey.

Keep the doctor away with apples and avocados.

Try these easy recipes.

CAULIFLOWER DELIGHT

If you have twenty minutes to spare, my most favorite dish is cauliflower soup. Take an organic cauliflower and break it into its florets. Cook them for ten minutes in a large pot with an inch or two of water (or broth) and a little butter. Ladle out the best-looking florets. Smash and whirl up the rest with an immersion blender, bind that with an egg yolk, and season with salt, pepper, and nutmeg. Put one floret per person in a bowl, pour the soup over it, and sprinkle with chives or green onion bits.

Delish.

CHICKPEA DELIGHT

Soak organic chickpeas in water overnight. Boil them for two hours to a soft consistency. Drain them and add garlic, lemon juice, olive oil, tahini, salt, and pepper. Put this all into the blender for a whirl until smooth. Hummus is ready.

Yummy.

TOMATO DELIGHT

Spread mayo on a slice of crusty bread. Top with thinly sliced onions and tomatoes. Salt. Pepper.

Fit for a king and a queen.

CHAPTER 6

F for **FORGIVENESS**

Free from Nag, Nag, Nag

"Forgiveness is not an occasional act. It is a constant attitude."
~ Martin Luther King Jr. ~

My long-planned visit with the dean of the medical school did not go so well. I was convinced I was a fine candidate, and I was ready to put in the work to become a physician. I had a PhD, not in biology, but still. I was a non-fiction published author and the manager of the university's Sleep Lab.

I asked the dean for advice on how best to proceed with my application. "How old are you? Thirty-four? Forget it. Too old. And you have a family? Raising two boys? The State expects at least thirty years of service out of you." He looked down at me with a triumphant condescending grin. I managed a polite goodbye.

Rejection. Humiliation. Insult. My age. My gender. My résumé—null. I felt wronged by this dean, this school, this state. I fumed. A poster on the wall behind the pompous dean's chair showed a cat dangling from a tree and written below, in large font: *Hang in there, baby. Friday is coming.* What an idiotic bureaucratic paper shuffler, I thought. He could at least have given me options. But there he was, stating his facts, all the while grinning with that grin. Hang in there, baby. What the hell.

Did I forgive that dean? Not for a while. But then, yes. I let go and changed course. I was blessed with a baby girl. A marvel. Years later, she would delight audiences with her music on the East and West Coasts, in the middle of the country, and in Europe, too. Thank you, Mr. Dean. And I forgave myself for not pushing the issue further.

Two thousand years ago, Seneca said, "Do not stumble over stones behind you." It's easy to waste time in an emotional prison of resentment over betrayal and disappointment. But we have a choice: either regurgitating old drama and ripping open wounds, or consciously letting go and focusing on how to find joy.

You may have done wrong. And that may gnaw on you. If you are haunted by regrets, if you think you should have done more in your life, assure yourself that you did all you could at the time. You had your reasons. Attention given to past events now does not change them. Stand tall. No need for torture. There is no glory in being Sisyphus with that boulder. Forgive yourself.

FORGIVENESS training:

Think of a specific issue that nags you.

Prepare to purge it from your life.

Take one hand, put it on the opposite shoulder.

With a resolute gesture, brush that bad memory off your sleeve.

Repeat it with the other hand on the other arm.

Do this three times.

Create space for you to fly free

CHAPTER 7

G for GARDENING

Hope in Action

"To get the best results, you must talk to your vegetables."
~ Prince Charles, now King Charles III ~

People who take care of plants live longer. They do. It's a proven fact. So, if you don't have one, get yourself a plant. If it dies, don't worry. Get another one. You'll be better at it. In my experience, here are the five hardiest house plants:

* **Jade**, a succulent, has leaves like polished coins; just saying the word succulent is fun

* **Monstera**, the cheese plant, makes holes in her huge leaves

* **Phalaenopsis**, an orchid, thrives on short soaking once a week and blooms for months

* **Pothos** or **devil's ivy** with heart-shaped leaves grows trailing vines

* **Spider plant** likes hanging from a hook; it grows its own babies on long stems

Gardening supports three Blue Zone people's habits: moderate exercise, stress reduction, and veggies for your plate. Squatting, bending, and digging is good for you. Connecting with your plants' needs gladdens the heart. Biting into your homegrown tomato satisfies the stomach. Everyone has green fingers. Yes. We wouldn't be here if we didn't.

Digging in soil is therapeutic. Putting your hands in the dirt calms and grounds you. There is an ancient, non-pathogenic bacteria that thrives in soil. Its name is *Mycobacterium vaccae*. When we touch and inhale it, it helps reduce stress and inflammation in our bodies. So, get your hands in some dirt. It's good for you. Dig in soil as often as you can. Grow these five easy herbs in the ground or in pots: basil, chives, dill, rosemary, and thyme. If you don't have a gardening space, consider getting a plot in a community garden together with a friend. It's a privilege to pull your weeds.

Gardening heals. In the United Kingdom, the National Health Service established a therapeutic gardening project called 'The London Grounding Project.' Run by a horticultural therapist and a clinical psychologist, the London Grounding Project is designed to alleviate severe mental health symptoms. Refugees and asylum seekers with post-traumatic stress disorder (PTSD) are invited to spend time gardening every week. Program participants report that taking care of plants helps them cope and find healing.

Gardening is about more than roses and radishes. Gardening is about cultivating the mind. *When* to plant, *what* to plant, and *where* improves cognitive functioning. As a gardener, you experience, hands on, the changing of the seasons. Thomas Berry, the cultural historian, religious scholar, and geologian (that's not a typo), called gardening *the active participation in the mysteries of the universe.* Like Eden, the most idyllic place before the snake showed up with the knowledge, any garden can inspire awe. Stroll in a garden and feel the wonder.

Because how a plant grows from the tiniest seed is a miracle. And so are you.

Tips

Organic gardening is the best. I heartily endorse organic gardening. No pesticides! My patch is poison-free.

Eggshells. I dry them, smash them, and scratch them into the soil. Unbelievably rich, they contain essential nutrients, like magnesium for chlorophyll production and enzyme usage, nitrogen for new growth, phosphorus for roots and blossoms, and potassium for photosynthesis and disease prevention. They're a treat for houseplants, too.

Coffee grounds. They feed microbes that promote good soil structure. Incorporating coffee grounds into the soil improves drainage and eliminates slugs. Worms love them, and happy worms make a healthy, aerated garden.

Create a pollinator garden with plants native to your area. Bees, large and small, will enthuse in their blooms. Butterflies, orange polka dotted and zebra-striped, will visit. And moths, espresso brown with white lines—they are pollinators too—will make your garden a happy place.

Dare food scaping guerilla style, for your pleasure. My home-owner association (the HOA) has strict rules against gardening. Yes. You read that right. The world is on the brink of climate disaster, and the HOA is against gardening. However, what they don't know won't make them angry. So, I hide my gardening in my landscaping. Into the midst of approved front yard decor, I throw seeds of edibles: arugula, basil, cilantro, dill, garlic chives, lettuce, mustard, and parsley. My crop is lush. Basil for pesto and dill for smoked salmon. Life is thriving along my driveway.

Experiment. Do something new every year. If you have the smallest spot of earth, plant elephant ears. Get them in the ground right after Mother's Day. Water daily and watch them unfold. Even with northern exposure, massive leaves of unequaled beauty will reward you all summer. Exotic, robust, tropical. With any luck, elephant ears even bloom for you. Next year, it could be twelve-foot sunflower towers.

Lastly, in the fall, don't rake. Shred and leave your leaves, they are the most precious fertilizer, and they're free. Your lawn will thank you.

GARDENING recommendations:

Befriend one plant today, and let it live with you.

Get yourself a window box.

Harvest rainwater.

Talk with your neighbors about four-season gardening.

Rebel against the HOA.

CHAPTER 8

H for HYDRATING

Cheers! Water it down.

"Water is the driving force in nature."
~ Leonardo da Vinci ~

Have you ever seen a neglected tomato plant in the heat of summer? It's not pretty. The plant becomes shriveled and sad. That's dehydration. We don't want to look or feel like that. Even *mild* dehydration can cause brain fog, confusion, cramps, dizziness, fatigue, and waning coordination. If you've made that $10,000 trip to the ER, like I have, you know the first thing they do is start a drip with fluids. Sometimes when there is a challenge in finding a vein, it's because of dehydration. So, hydrate properly.

Twenty to thirty percent of older adults are chronically dehydrated. When *you* feel thirsty, your body is begging you for water. However, as we age, our ability to sense thirst can decrease, and our bodies may store less water. So, it's critically important to drink water, even if you are not thirsty.

Thirsty or not, eight glasses a day are recommended. That's eight glasses of *water*, not soft drinks or fruit juices. It may seem like a lot, but the National Institute of Health (NIH) has found that well-hydrated adults live longer. So, drink up. You need even more if you enjoy a Sunday sauna. Water means life. Hydration is easy and so simple. It's in our control. It's best to measure the daily intake. In order not to fool myself-as has happened in the past-I now fill a pitcher with eight cups of water in the morning and drink it down as my day goes on.

The benefits of drinking water are as infinite as the ocean. And yes, you will need to pee more often. That's part of the point: you are flushing out toxins. Less toxins means better brain function, better digestion, and more energy. Drinking water minimizes the possibility of headaches and kidney stones. If you drink a glass of water thirty minutes before each meal, it helps fill your stomach. We can lose some weight just from drinking water. If and when enjoying alcohol, it is highly recommended to have one glass of water for every boozy drink. It helps then and the next day, too. Make eight glasses of water a day your habit. Your body and brain will thank you.

HYDRATING encouragement:

Set up three hydration stations: one in your kitchen, bedroom, and car.

Have cups always full of water.

When you are on the go, say no to plastic. Take a refillable bottle instead.

Stop and be grateful for water.

CHAPTER 9

I for INDEPENDENCE

Living on Your Terms

"Independence is happiness."
~ Susan B. Anthony ~

Maintain your independence fiercely. You've found YOUR freedom and the beauty in it. Do all you can to keep it. Do not quit doing what you love. Over time you may have to modify the *how* as your body changes. But *no* stopping! Self-sufficiency is a power to enjoy and to maintain.

I love downhill skiing. Been skiing in the Alps since I was eighteen. For every foot we skied down, we had to walk uphill on seal skins strapped to our skis. There were no lifts for people—only for luggage up to the cabin. Tow ropes and T-bars, if you were lucky. But hey! During Covid, I did not ski, and when the dangers were over, I hesitated to get back into it. I had apprehension and a bit of anxiety. My kids offered to ski with me, which I appreciated, but declined. They enjoy super steep, double black diamond slopes, and I prefer smooth blue and green runs. Skiing alone was not an option, but decades of happy skiing memories with family and friends nudged me not to give up. So, I enrolled in ski school.

What did I find there? Lots of fun in the sun with a new social group half my age as I started a new skiing history. Lighter, without the weight of and wait for a husband whose schedule I had to mind. No expectations of praise. No complaining. It was just me, the hill, the sun, and the snow. Liberated! Liberated is how I felt in the company of strangers. It was AWESOME. I fell twice and was grateful to be helped back up. Then, after being steadied, I outskied my newbie fellow students, swinging down the slope, loving every minute of it and smiling all the way down. The teacher called me, *show off*. Yes! Thank you.

Independence starts at home. If you like where you live, keep your place. Benjamin Franklin wrote, "Old folks and old trees, if you remove them, it's ten to one that you kill them." Stay in your home as long as you are able. Are adjustments done as you need them, to keep you happy and able to function there? Throw out tripping hazards, like carpets, or secure them properly. Always put shoes away. Know where your pet is, especially in the dark. Install safety grips. They can be made of nice wood. Use night lights. However, practice to feel your way around in the dark with eyes closed . . . just in case. Know where candles and matches are. Keep your space organized and clean. A bonus is that cleaning counts as exercise.

If you need repairs, make a plan to do them. It may seem daunting, but a reward is waiting. Get at least two estimates for any job, three if you can. Check the reviews of whom you may hire. Pay only half up front, never more. When the job is well done, pay in full. Be an angel of patience holding the carrot: the second half of the payment.

Be in charge of your emotional and physical health. Laugh a lot with people who like to laugh. Get regular medical and dental checkups. Choose a team of healthcare providers with different specialties to keep you in shape. Get second opinions. Speak your mind. Voice your concerns. Arrive at your medical appointments with your questions in hand and insist they be answered. Identify an ally who will advocate on your behalf if you are hospitalized. Consider alternative healing options. As with everything, be diligent in your research. There are different ways to approach healing. Countries with socialized medicine favor homeopathic methods and natural ways of healing nationwide. It works for them. Prevention is their emphasis, not disease.

Be in charge of your financial health. Understand your money and how to best use it for your needs. Balance income and expenses. Living within your means is satisfying because it reduces stress.

Maintain your style of living. Keep doing what feels good to *you*. Order the pizza *you* like. Get Botox if you want it. Go gray if you like. Yes, gentlemen, gray is handsome for you, too. Be extravagant with flowers. Get out of the house daily. Stay in the rhythm of how you get around. It's empowering. Depending on your situation, use public transportation. Uber drivers are almost everywhere. Take the car for a spin. Keep driving regularly, as long as it is safely possible. If you like to trim your bushes, yes you can do so, but maybe not with a chainsaw-like gadget. I did that once, got carried away, and cut the cord. Thank goodness it was not my foot.

Ask for help when needed. Build a resource file of professionals who can assist you. Have it current to avoid a crisis. Your list might include assistance with deep cleaning, an electrician, a handy person, a lawn service, and a plumber. They all support your independence, keeping YOU in control. Have a trusted neighbor keep a key to your place, as a precaution.

INDEPENDENCE practice:

Change one thing in your home to make it safer.

Check all lightbulbs.

Make a monthly budget of income and expenses.

Treat yourself.

Celebrate.

CHAPTER 10

J for JOY

The Elixir of the Soul

"Freude, schöner Götterfunken, Tochter aus Elysium
Joy, Beautiful Divine Spark, Daughter from Heaven"
~ Ode to Joy — Ninth Symphony — Ludwig van Beethoven ~

Joy cultivates well-being. Joy is . . . well . . . joyous. Joyous people live longer.

However, what to do when there is no joy anywhere at a particular moment, only anxiousness, despondency, and sadness?

Sometimes, when I feel like that, I ask myself, *what could make me happy in the next five minutes? What? WHAT?* **WHAT?** And I manage to find things that bring me joy when I stop and focus on what has brought me joy in the past. You can come up with something, too. It can be small or big. Just try it. The best thing is to practice giving yourself joy. Repeat doing those things or being with people who have brought it. Could there be joy in . . .

* Binging on your favorite TV series, or movie

* Blueberries with honey yogurt

* Calling your best friend to talk, talk, talk

* Calling a long-lost friend to talk, talk, talk
* Chocolate cake with whipped cream
* Coloring in a coloring book
* Creating a tasty meal from stuff in the fridge
* Digging in soil
* Driving your car
* Fishing
* Fixing that motor
* Getting out of the house, simple as that
* Helping someone
* Lighting a fire
* Line dancing to the tune "All My Exes Live in Texas"
* Kayaking
* Knitting
* Meditating
* Napping
* Nothing—doing absolutely nothing
* Planting a crepe myrtle bush
* Playing the ukulele
* Polishing your mother's silver
* Praying
* Primal screaming
* A puzzle

❋   Reading that naughty novel

❋   Shopping for favorite things

❋   Shredding the hell out of old documents

❋   Smoked trout with sliced cucumbers, fresh dill, and loads of sour cream

❋   Soaking in a hot tub

❋   Solitaire

❋   Star gazing

❋   Tennis

❋   Turning on your favorite music

❋   A walk in the woods

❋   Wine—a lovely glass of wine

Can you think of more? Make joy your habit.

If none of this snaps you out of the funk, remember your morning routine: filling your brain and heart with thoughts and feelings of gratitude. It is your good fortune to be alive on this day. Gratitude and fear do not live in the same heart.

JOY — some ideas to try out:

Say out loud what gives you joy now.

Share that with someone dear.

Dance to your favorite tune.

The most joyful moment in my life was . . .

CHAPTER 11

K for KNOWING

The Quest of the Ages

"The man who asks a question is a fool for a minute.
The man who does not ask is a fool for life."
~ Confucius ~

The ancient Greeks built the Temple of Apollo in the city of Delphi 2,500 years ago. At that time, Delphi was considered the navel of the world, their religious and cultural center. The Apollo Temple was home to the famous Oracle of Delphi. Pilgrims, diplomats, and heads of state from all over the world came to get advice for private and public matters. Before embarking on his campaign to conquer Persia, Alexander the Great sought her council, too. The Oracle declared, *you are invincible.* Alexander went to defeat Darius III, King of Persia. Today, Delphi is a UNESCO World Heritage Site.

Into that temple's limestone, the ancient Greeks hammered three phrases. Three guiding principles that were paramount to them. Are they still applicable today? You bet. Some things never change. The first of the three is:

Know Thyself

What an invitation! Understand ourselves. What is our nature? What are we like at our core? What is our essence? What makes us click? What?

At any age, it is important to know what is best for us. The more we know ourselves, the better we can focus on what we need, the easier it is to allow time and space to refine ourselves with regular personal check-ins as we change and as life happens.

Know your body. Observe what your body wants. Ask it and listen to it. If your body wants a nap, lie down. If your body wants asparagus, it wants asparagus. If your body wants cheesy grits, fix it for dinner (or breakfast if you like). Cherries? Yes. Your body knows.

Know your limits. One day, I was in a rush, eager to meet two friends at happy hour. My dog took a bit longer than usual to clear her channels, so I hurried. I put on my favorite decorations and dashed out of the house. I had a lovely, refreshing time. When I got home, I noticed I had worn two different earrings. It was an unintended fashion statement; a first for me!

I rush less these days. And that's okay. I now give myself ample time. I want to be at the airport with an hour to spare, so I do it. I get there nice and early. If you like the rush of being tight with time, start fifteen minutes later than you think you should. Everybody is different.

Know your dreams and desires. If you want to learn things you never thought of before, satisfy that drive. If you yearn to do new things, explore. If you want to accomplish just that one thing, work on it every day. Even ten minutes a day can make an impact.

A cool way to discover your innermost makeup, if you are inclined to find out, is the Gallup Clifton Strengths Test. You can take it online. The test asks you to rate your level of agreement with a series of statements regarding thirty-four themes. From there it figures out your five dominant strengths. Bingo. It was bullseye and total fun for me. My top strength came out as liking harmony. Yes. True. I do like harmony. Maybe taking that test can be a revelation for you, too.

The other two maxims of the wise ancients are:

 # 2: Nothing in Excess

Moderation in all things, even moderation in moderation.

 # 3: Surety Brings Ruin

Be aware of the dangers of false certainty.

KNOWING exercises:

What would you ask the Oracle of Delphi if you had the chance?

Take the Gallup Clifton Strengths Test.

Look in the mirror and love yourself the way you are.

Tell your body that you appreciate it.

CHAPTER 12
L for LISTS

Your Private Butler and Motivator

"We make lists because we don't want to die."
~ Umberto Eco ~

I love lists. I make one almost every day. Having *to-do* items on paper is soothing, especially when life feels overwhelming. My list waits for me by the coffee pot in the morning. It serves as a framework for my day.

I recommend lists. Your day will not be empty. The list gives you control. You are in charge. When an idea comes, write it down. Immediately. Have pads and pencils around the house, even in the laundry room, or take notes on your phone (if you can find it). Prioritize the list if you like.

Your list can be a catch-all for the unpleasant things you don't want to do; things you hate or worry about. To make them disappear from your life, write them down. Once formulated, find the nerve to take care of one of them before 10:00 a.m. Call about that pesky, unexpected price increase in internet service. Have it explained, removed, or adjusted. Do it with a light heart. Kick ass. Delete it from the list and go on with your day.

The list liberates. It keeps the brain available for more interesting stuff. Produced from your PLANNING self, the list frees up your DREAMING self and offers room to create. The list gives you peace of mind.

The list is a motivator. It promises feel-good moments and a sense of accomplishment when you check things off. Sometimes I cross them out twice using different pens, doubling the pleasure. Savor your accomplishments, big or small. As Voltaire said, "The pursuit of pleasure must be the goal of every rational person."

The list keeps you centered on what's important. When you feel tired or uncertain about what is next, the list can give you a second wind. Put on Mozart or Elton John, or whatever music you like, have some pineapple (it's high in antioxidants), drink your eighth glass of water, and you will find the energy for one more thing, like texting a friend good night. That's on *my* list.

The list jogs your memory. It can serve as your private daily cognitive trainer. As you are going to sleep at night, it helps to review your day. Think about what you did, the people you spoke to, and what new things you learned.

Every week, I declare one day *my* day; a NOD: a **N**o **O**bligation **D**ay. A day off. No list. Blessed nothingness. Try it and see what happens. Can you stand it? All week, you may be looking forward to it.

LIST suggestions:

Choose a spot in your place to park your daily list.

Have a pen sitting right there.

Afford a fresh page every day.

The spiral notebook gets a second wind by using it backward.

Enjoy your deletes.

CHAPTER 13

M for MOVING

The Fountain of Youth

"To keep the body in good health is a duty, otherwise,
we shall not be able to keep our mind strong and clear."
~ Buddha ~

M ovement is vital for healthy aging. Movement is miraculous in what it does for us. Movement gets the blood pumping, and it encourages us to go on.

There are many ways to move. Stand up at least once an hour if you sit for extended periods of time. Give your body a movement break. Bend. Reach. Squat. It's very important. Stoop. Stretch. Do it with enthusiasm. It's good for you. You could bike, garden, play ping-pong, pickleball, row, run, swim, do Tai Chi, vacuum with vigor, or do yoga—even in a chair or on a wall. Turn on the music and dance.

I made a commitment to myself to walk every day. Cold or hot weather. Rain or shine. Snow or fog. The people of Iceland say, and I found it to be true, "There is no bad weather, only bad clothing." Walking is easy on the joints, is always available, and it's free. A walk of any length is terrific. Walk in the moment. Experience the moment. I recommend that you, too, make walking a daily routine first thing in the morning, or second thing after coffee, or later if you are a night person. Alone or with a friend. Or a dog. Or both. Not every day is easy, but hey! Muster the will to get out! The good news is that minor aches can often be walked off.

I head out with my head up, shoulders straight, imagining a searchlight beaming from my chest. Keeping a straight posture, I give my lungs a chance to expand. Sometimes, I focus on my breathing, like in a walking meditation practice, inhaling for four steps, holding it for four, breathing out for four steps, and holding it for four. I can do that only briefly because I get distracted. I vary my speed. I walk backward for a bit. That straightens my back and exercises different muscles. I roll my shoulders, like paddling in a kayak. I give myself a big hug. No one's looking. Even if they are, who cares? The newest thing is rucking, where you carry weights in a backpack to strengthen bones and muscles. That's a bit too much for me but may be quite okay for you.

Walking is a way to harvest ideas. The movement shakes them loose. Movement activates antennae that catch ideas from the universe. For my walks, I tuck paper and a pencil in my pocket. Once an idea is written down, I'm free to receive another one. When Beethoven took his walks, he carried a notebook with him to capture motifs for his symphonies.

Walking resets my mood. I chat with my neighbors. I get to know the solo walkers and the dog walkers. Being exposed to a world larger than myself—to birds, clouds, trees, wind, the blue immensity above, and the always present stars—I come home with new resolve.

Walking is amazing for the mind and for the brain. Flexibility in the body holds hands with flexibility in the brain. At a Society of Biological Psychiatry Convention cocktail party, I once asked a young Stanford University neurologist the question, "How does one prevent Alzheimer's?"

Without hesitation, she said, "Three twenty-minute walks a day."

Move your body with weights. My friend Pat loves to lift them. Lots of pounds. Six days a week. That would bore me to death, but everybody's got their thing. Weight training encourages balance and builds muscles. Gaining muscles benefits your bones, metabolism, and mental sharpness. So, I really should do it, too.

You've probably heard of the concept that you need 10,000 steps a day. Science recommends only 6,000 to 7,000 steps for cardiovascular health. So why a whopping 10,000? A Japanese pedometer company chose as their logo the Japanese character for *10,000* (*ichiman*) which resembles a person walking. This branding was taken as the truth, and now 10,000 steps a day is a thing (that's a clever linguistic visual joke). I grab any opportunity to sneak in extra steps. I leave my car at the far end of the parking lot. I take the stairs when feasible. I add an evening stroll. Counting my steps every day is rewarding.

"You've got the body of a sixty-year-old," the massage therapist in Breckenridge, Colorado, told me on my ski vacation.

"No way," I said. "I'm eighty. Could it be the walking?"

She said, "Keep doing it."

Be sure to use your hands. Hand movements stimulate the brain. Build a shelf. Carry your groceries. Crochet. Cut veggies. Do the crossword in pencil. Knit. Macrame. Mend. Paint the baseboards—two coats. Paint on canvas. Play an instrument. Repair stuff. Sew. Squeeze the railing every time you take the stairs. Write with a pen. Try calligraphy.

Warm up to MOVING:

Set yourself a daily movement goal that you can measure.

Get a buddy to do it with you.

Join a sports club for motivation.

CHAPTER 14

N for NATURE

Get Outside

"Study nature, love nature, stay close to nature. It will never fail you."
~ Claude Monet ~

I marvel at what goes on in my bird café, a feeding station attached with suction cups to my window. It's popular with Hollywood finches, flashy cardinals, dark-eyed juncos, downy woodpeckers, and bluebirds. They visit in the mornings, afternoons, and evenings. Fat squirrels show up also. They park themselves in the feeder until their tummies are full, occasionally wrecking it by bringing the whole thing down with their jumping extravaganzas. One spring morning, I walked into my study to find two birds sitting in my feeder, one fat, fluffy, and plump, the other a slender adult sparrow who was filling the youngster's beak with one seed after the other. And then some. Enjoying my yummy supply in leisure and safety. It was a beautiful thing to watch.

My interactions with birds boost my mood. I open the window or go outside to watch and listen. I witness the sweetness in the ways young birds imitate their parents, particularly how they learn and repeat song sequences, first tentatively, then with confidence. It motivates me and cheers me up. I found an app and now use it to identify the endearing singers.

Flowers connect me to nature. I just love flowers. Being in their presence is essential to my well-being. There is a reason why they show up at any affair of importance: weddings, funerals, anniversaries, holidays, birthdays, world conferences, and at your table. Flowers offer unquestioned beauty, goodness, harmony, and perfection; some call it godliness. Flowers carry meaning outside of the rational experience. They connect us to what the ancients called *anima mundi*: the soul of the world. Having flowers around just makes one feel good.

Shinrin-yoku is a Japanese word for forest bathing. Yes, forest bathing. Isn't that marvelous? Not hiking, jogging, or exercising in the woods. It means walking or sitting under trees, soaking in their calmness, and inhaling their essential oils. James Lundie in my book's theme song, "For the Trees," puts it this way:

> *Without trees there are no glades*
> *Sacred groves or dappled shade*
> *When the days are long . . .*
> *Standing firm and growing tall*
> *They have watched and seen us all*
> *Traveling our paths*
> *And like their radiating rings*
> *That translate time to solid things*
> *They warm our hearts and hearths.*

Listen to the song on my website: www.joyouslongevity.com.

Trees connect what's above with what's below. They communicate through their interwoven roots to survive. With resilience, patience, and adaptability to the seasons, they stretch their branches to the sky, waiting for the sun. In storms, they bend and thrash and then return to stillness. We can learn much from them. The Trillion Tree Campaign counters climate change with planting one trillion trees to do us and the Earth some good.

Being in nature for two to three hours a week is proven to boost mental health, reducing the stress hormone cortisol. Sunlight prompts our skin to make vitamin D, which is good for our bones. Sunlight encourages our brain to produce serotonin, a feel-good chemical, for a better mood. Visit your neighborhood park, a state park, or a national park. Frequent a botanical garden. Get out into the wild, to a nature preserve, a lake, the ocean, the mountains. Nature nurtures, gives comfort, and inspires awe. Mythology speaks of spirits inhabiting trees and plants, giving them consciousness. How does that make you feel? What does that make you think about?

I think of the universe and our role in it. We all are taking part in nature, just like the birds, the flowers, and the trees. Consider nature's cycles. Consider the seasons. Four times a year we celebrate them with special bonfires: in June, on the summer solstice, the longest day; in December, on the winter solstice, when the light starts to come back; and on the spring and fall equinoxes. A fire is a primal way to connect with nature's energy. Does that make you think about how *you* change with the seasons, mentally, physically, and emotionally? Love nature and it will love you back.

You can draw upon NATURE's energy:

Go for a picnic in the park.

Hug your favorite tree.

Soak in the sunset.

Watch the wonder of a starry night in the desert.

Say out loud with Mary Oliver, the poet, *Glory to the rose and the leaf, to the seed, to the silverfish. Glory to time and the wild fields, and to joy.*

CHAPTER 15

O for OBJECTS

Lighten the Load

"Believe what your heart tells you
when you ask, does this spark joy?"
~ Marie Kondo ~

S tuff.
  Do I *really* want all the stuff I have? Do my kids want it? Do friends want it? Who on Earth wants it? Anyone? What gives it value?

The ordinary American home houses an astounding number of objects—an average of 300,000. That's not counting the contents in off-site storage. Do you love all the objects you possess? Do you like them? Do you need them? They take up a lot of room. What do you possess that's a burden for you to maintain? Maybe it's time to let certain items go.

Ask each object if it brings you joy. If it doesn't, get rid of it. Such action takes hard thinking, and it can be intense, but it's worth it. That black, precious St. John's knit suit in your closet, the one with the fine collar, the gold buttons, and the tight skirt, the suit you tried to impress your partner with, the garment that, by just looking at it, now makes you miserable? Out with it! Donate it along with the bag that enshrined the darn thing. High five.

Start a new phase of lighter living with less stuff. What you have not used in a while, you probably don't need. Five sets of dishes? Twelve glass vases? Thirty T-shirts? Pare back on the number of objects you own just like a gardener prunes back the fruit on apple and peach trees. Too much fruit encourages pests and makes the branches break. Declutter! There is less to trip over, less to dust, less to irritate you, and more space to display the beautiful objects you genuinely love.

My attic was crowded with baby skis, a beer can collection, comic books, college manuals, sawhorses, a tent, wrestling trophies, and more. It also housed a silver Yamaha trumpet in a brown case with blue velvet lining. This was my oldest son's trumpet. He does not play it anymore and he does not want it shipped to him. So, what now? Keep it? I remember sitting in the school stadium with his younger brother and sister, trying to make out who he was in the marching band down on the football field. All the trumpeters looked alike in their uniforms. These were our Friday nights way back when. And here I am at eighty with his trumpet. Nostalgia? No and yes. But it's time to lighten the load. Time for this trumpet to get a new life. My local music store offered a donation program, allowing high school students to borrow or rent the instrument. What a joy to repurpose.

Take on your OBJECTS:

Set the timer for fifteen minutes to go through your stuff.

Open one drawer and get rid of what you don't need.

Inspect one kitchen cabinet and make room.

Do it today.

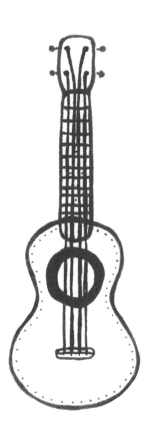

CHAPTER 16

P for **PURPOSE**

Why You Are Here

*"I firmly believe that we all need to find something to
do in our lives, that stops us from eating the couch."*
~ Elizabeth Gilbert ~

Do you have a sense of purpose? The answer is yes. Why?
Because we *all* have a purpose. You may have to rediscover
what it is, but you are here on planet Earth for a reason.

When I explored that question, I found that my purpose is
to share with others what I have learned to be useful. One way
I'm fulfilling my purpose is by writing this book. I worked on it
daily, did research, and experimented with various formats. This
project required deadlines, which worked for me because I could
measure my progress with each editing round. It empowered
me. Doing this book caused me to evaluate my own life. Helping
my reader deal with aging created calmness, comfort, and ease
of mind for me. That gave me a sense of fulfillment. Is there
something *you* can do that will do the same for you?

Purpose can be found in small things. Like going fishing,
maintaining the perfect lawn, paddle boarding, and crafting

things. That can give purpose. My friend in Florida finds purpose in staying agile enough to walk his puppy dog up and down the sand dunes twice a day. If on your bucket list is to parachute out of an airplane, begin training for it. Getting in shape for this gives you purpose. A trip to the store for items you want can give the morning purpose. In some parts of the world, people go to the market every day, for the freshest food and to catch up on the latest news. The deeper purpose of going to the market is to interact with friends.

Purpose can be found in big things. Caring for parents, a partner, children, grandchildren, or a pet is a purpose. So is taking care of yourself by cultivating a healthy lifestyle.

My friend Pat calls shows for the blind and the visually impaired. She describes what happens during theatre performances for persons who have trouble seeing. Through hearing her words on their headsets, they can enjoy spectacles like Broadway plays, classic movies with a live orchestra, and outdoor musicals. The equipment she needs is heavy and delicate. Resiliently, she schlepps the gear into the venues and up to the broadcast booths. She is passionate about helping. That gives her purpose.

My next-door neighbor finds purpose in keeping people connected. She loves to plan gatherings of all kinds. Whether it be Bastille Day, Cinco de Mayo, Octoberfest, Saint Patrick's Day, progressive dinners, or a life celebration, she plans a gathering. Covid did not stop her. During that time of deep isolation and fear, she created a daily ritual for us neighbors, which proved to be a ray of hope for all of us. EVERY evening at 5:00 p.m. in the winter and at 6:00 p.m. in the summer, she invited us to meet outside at the end of her driveway, taking full safety precautions, with masks and proper distancing of chairs. If it rained there were texts. In the cold, her husband lit a fire. These gatherings became a meaningful way to check in for us all.

When I see images of retirement folks lounging on a beach with a margarita, I dismiss that as a made-up sentiment created by TV ad agencies. It's great for a couple of weeks maybe, but then what? You have skills and experience. Why not use them? Why not work? For real life, consider a part-time position that ties in with doing what you love *and* possibly earning some money. Extra money is always good. Working keeps you involved with people. You could maybe consider working as a consultant of some kind, a mentor, a park ranger, a substitute teacher, or an usher.

For PURPOSE, trust your intuition:

Search your soul, listen to it, and declare a purpose.

Put that purpose at the center of your life.

This is what I like to do, and it is for . . . (fill in the blank).

Look forward to it every day.

CHAPTER 17

Q for QUIETUDE

Essential to Unplug

"Sitting quietly, doing nothing, spring comes,
and the grass grows by itself."
~ Zen Proverb ~

Computer crashes, conspiracy theories, Facebook hackings, gossip, Instagram, mobile pings, prank calls, Tik Tok, Twitter, TV news. Noise. Noise. Noise.

It's time to unplug.

At least three times a day, stop and give yourself an intentional moment. Be only with yourself. Hang out with you. Drop your shoulders. Close your eyes. Feel some gratitude. Being still slows down your heart rate.

Meditation is an excellent enhancer for quietude. It's practiced in many ways. It can be deep, slow, square breathing:

Breathe in, 2, 3, 4

Hold 2, 3, 4

Breathe out 2, 3, 4

Hold 2, 3, 4

I have a challenging time with this kind of meditation practice because I don't have the patience, yet. But I'm working on it. Katherine May made the point that meditation was most likely invented by the male gender, who could sit for a long time undisturbed. I find that something to think about.

I practice other ways of daily quietude. I check in with my buddleia butterfly bushes, admiring their flowers. I gaze at a candle, listen to music, repeat a mantra, read poetry, or I say a prayer in the middle of the night when inquietude pops up.

I try daydreaming, where I let my mind go wherever it wants. Long ago when I was little, in the afternoons, my mother and I would look out the wide open window from the third floor of our apartment building, arms on the windowsill, watching the street below, the trees on the hills across the vista, and the clouds. That was her way of experiencing quietude. It is a treasured memory that I have of being with her.

My quietude comes from grounding; having skin contact with the earth. I walk barefoot on grass, absorbing energy from the ground. Standing on earth connects me with the planet's electrical power. I keep a properly grounded grounding mat under my desk. It mimics the electrical current of the earth. I notice our pit bull Mary loves lying on it. She likes grounding, too.

At the start of my evening, I like to play solitaire. I admire the sunset. It takes the sun four minutes from touching the horizon to going under. Before bedtime, to wrap up my day, I sometimes sit outside on my kitchen deck in the dark with a sip of whisky and look at the stars.

The quietest moment I ever had was on a recent trip to Southern France, on a remote mountaintop above the small village of Les Aires. On a sunny day in September, we drove up a very narrow gravel track (if a car came down at that time, OMG, a logistical nightmare) going to the ancient ruins of the Chateau de Mourcairol, one of the oldest castles in France. This place was first mentioned in the testament of the Vicomte de Bézier in 990 AD. We parked and climbed the steep, perilous trail—no railings, no signs, no sound. On top of the crag, we were grandly rewarded with a spectacular view of the Languedoc area and the structure of a small Romanesque chapel. Dedicated to the archangel Saint Michel, this chapel has been here for over a thousand years.

Leafy fans of lush iris plants guarded the entrance. The simple wooden door was wide open. In the Catholic religion, Michel, the saint, has the power to protect against evil. However, before Christ and the Bible's angels showed up, the Romans worshipped their god Mercury here, and before them, the Celts also held this place sacred. That adds another thousand years or more of humans cherishing this site as HOLY. Why did they choose this place? Why? What did the ancients know? What esoteric knowledge did they have to pick this rocky outcrop as their sacred site?

Maybe the earth has unusual energies here. Maybe humans since way back connected with such power. Could I tap into it, I wondered?

On intuition, inside the chapel, I laid flat on my back on one of the low, narrow, hard, gnarly, plank-like wood benches. With hands and bare feet hanging down, I touched the ancient stones on the floor. Open chest, open mind, totally exposed to what could happen, I closed my eyes and listened to the silence of centuries enshrining the mystery of this place. A feeling of peace flooded me, convincing me that things would be alright.

Granted, this was a very unique way to experience quietude. We surely can find a familiar place to be quiet in our bodies, in our heads, and in our hearts.

Take on QUIETUDE:

Choose a time.
Find a place where you feel blessed, not stressed.
Your church, your garden.
Your mosque, your synagogue.
The woods.
The mountains.
The sea.
Be still.

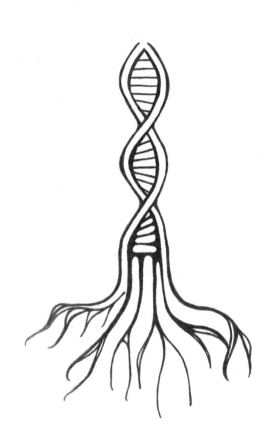

CHAPTER 18

R for ROOTS

Cozy with Your DNA

"The cosmos is within us. We are made of star stuff."
~ Carl Sagan ~

B eing an immigrant by choice, to whom everything feels more precious in the new country, I rarely get feelings about having lost my roots. I love living in the US, but then, a longing to revisit the place of my childhood emerged—memories of continental summers that heated the pavement under my bare feet, slices of hearty bread with butter, the garden where freshly picked pears would ripen in piles to their full aroma inside the summer cottage made of blonde wood. Such yearnings were tainted with an apprehension of possibly finding a mess. I left more than seventy years ago.

To be at peace with myself, I took a chance. Together with my daughter and son-in-law, I took a cruise on the river Elbe. One of the stops was the city of Meissen, where I was born.

I come from blacksmiths, farmers, music and home economics teachers, railroaders, seamstresses, tailors, and a theatre critic. They all lived in Saxony, Germany. Way back in the fifth century, my Saxon ancestors roamed all over Europe, as far north as England. Still today, the saying goes that Saxons like to travel and that, in Saxony, beautiful girls grow on trees.

On that cruise, we had three precious hours off the boat. Early in the morning, we wanted a taxi, but the ship concierge discouraged us. *This is the former East. Things don't work here like they do in the West.* OMG. The wall fell in 1989, more than thirty years ago, when the two Germanies reunited. What would we find?

My mouth got dry, my stomach queasy. I remembered way back when the sky burned red from the fire-bombing of Dresden, a town only fifteen miles up the river. I remembered hiding from Russian soldiers in the pantry in the company of women whose faces were painted with ashes—the pantry door barricaded by a wardrobe. I remembered New Year's Eve, 1948. World War II had ended three years before. I was seven when my mother and I left this place with only a green handcart and a backpack. She gave up everything, her home, her family, her history, to get us out of the Russian-occupied East to join my father in the West. Just five feet tall, it was my mother's energy that made her a pure power. Her blue eyes were fully open from the time she got up. She focused on options, potential, and truth. While the rest of her family sleepwalked through the dangers, the propaganda, and the tyranny instituted by the Soviets, she took action. She knew people at the East-West border, who helped with the escape. They were familiar with the schedule of the armed border patrol. At midnight, during a shift change, the barbed wire fence would be unguarded for fifteen minutes and the soldiers were carelessly drunk. This was our window to slip through. In the freezing cold. On a full moon. And we did.

Now I was back.

"Don't worry." My kids took the lead. "Let's find your old address and see. However, and whatever it is, we are here with you."

We found the tree-lined street. My three-story apartment building was still there. Oh, the delight to see the place. What a relief to feel joy. New windows. New paint. A for-rent sign. The doors to my place were locked, so we 'broke into' the attached house next door, which had the same layout as mine. We walked up three flights, and I teared up. So many good memories came to me, like dinners in the room reserved for special occasions; like the mysterious cabinet in the hallway with its locked treasures of crayons, pencils, and colored paper; like the balcony inside the staircase, opening onto an airy courtyard, three stories high, with beautifully painted gold ornaments. My mother kept pink cyclamens in a window box way back when.

Back outside, we walked the thousand steps to the top of the vineyard and found our allotment in the *Schrebergarten* (the community garden). My mother had planted tobacco for my father when he would return from the war. The *Klapsliebling* pear tree still stood there, stout, strong, and lush with fruit. Could it be the same tree after so many years? My tree? I grabbed a pear and it *fell* into my hand. Round, smooth, and juicy.

Narrow cobblestone passages led us to the Albrechtsburg, the city's gothic castle with its cathedral. I remembered sitting here on the ground in the sun in the square. It was the summer of 1946. All of the women in town were mandated with cleaning and salvaging stones from the bombed out ruins for reconstruction. I still felt their heavy silence and heard the click, click, click of the hammers.

We had enough time for a short castle tour. To protect the dark wooden floors, we had to take off our shoes. Invited to wear huge felt slippers, we glided and skated through the grand hall, adorned with paintings of its past glory, among them long-bearded heroes and their fine long-skirted ladies. Eight hundred years ago, pageantry par excellence happened here; it was power and party central. Now there was even a gift shop.

Back on the boat, I felt glad to have found beauty. But this *coming home* made me realize that my roots were no longer there. I had left for good. I felt like a tourist. I had always wanted to get out of Germany because I could not deal with the guilt of my country's history. Getting away as far as I could from the Soviet threat was an added bonus. I have grown new roots in the US. I love it here.

Ideas for ROOTS:

Check out *your* ancestry.

Find *your* geographical roots.

Go visit

Stay a while.

CHAPTER 19

S for **SOCIALIZING**

The Life Saver

"In nature, nothing exists alone."
~ Rachel Carson ~

In 2018, then British Prime Minister Theresa May established a Ministry for Loneliness. Britain is the first government to formally recognize the devastating effects of isolation. Loneliness is a global phenomenon, more dangerous than depression. Loneliness can shorten the lifespan by up to fifteen years. To extend our lives, we must be social. It's vital.

Reaching out is the ticket to well-being. Have happy hour at least once a week and invite people to it. Watch sports with a friend at the local pub, or better yet, get out to a live event. Join an arts club, an athletic club, a book club, a garden club, an investment club, a movie club, or a Scrabble club. Take the opportunity to make new friends. Make phone dates with friends and family; Zoom or Facetime or WhatsApp or whatever. Call. Text. Email. Send messages. Write. Reach out. It will extend or even save your life.

I do 'Soup on Sundays.' It's an event of ultimate comfort. I prepare two soups, the ones I enjoy making. One in the crockpot and one on the stove. My guests bring bread, dessert, and wine. To be gourmet is not the point, but to be easy, stress free, and relaxed. We avoid serious conversations about religion and politics. Our gatherings are for comfort and safety. Try this once a month with family, neighbors, and friends. I tidy up a bit, but not too much; I don't want to scare my guests. A beverage loosens the vibe. Maybe create a specialty drink with an irreverent name. Would you like another one? Cheers.

Sharing a cup of tea is an international classic. The word *tea* or *cha* features in 90 percent of the world's languages. Tea drinkers live longer. I once attended a high tea in Bangkok and enjoyed savory and sweet delights loaded onto five-tiered crystal towers: cheeses, chocolate pralines, curds, custards, fruit tarts, quiches, sandwiches, scones, and tortes . . . all kinds of tortes. Everything was extravagant and lush. But I say less is more. Do not make too much fuss. When you are truly relaxed, your guests will be too. Heat the kettle, stick tea bags in some cups, and pour the hot water. Have sugar and milk, cake, or cookies, either homemade or from the store. Cucumber sandwiches with mayo would be extra special. Sit. Sip. Talk. Listen. It's about connecting. Bask in the joy of being with the people you like.

Choose a daily check-in partner. Hello! Wellness check. After my husband died, and I lived alone, it was a comfort. It still is—my friend and I keep it going. Make a list of family members and favorite people to keep in touch with regularly: daily, once a week, or twice a month.

A very special way of socializing happens to me every day. During the pandemic, my daughter and her husband decided to rent out their place in Los Angeles and move in with me. They transformed my storage space into a state-of-the-art recording studio. The three of us are part of a rising trend: multigenerational family living. On my little street alone there are three multigenerational households. Cooking, eating, and cleaning up together, sharing ideas, learning from each other, teasing, and relying on each other. My house is active with creativity. It's a lot of fun. We live better together in a new forcefield of care.

For SOCIALIZING:

Enrich your life with a new connection.

Refresh an old connection.

Open your home.

Open your heart.

Party.

CHAPTER 20

T for TRAVEL

Wooing the Unexpected

*"The real voyage of discovery consists not in seeing
new landscapes, but in having new eyes."*
~ Marcel Proust ~

Travel is an investment in yourself. And an investment in yourself is a way to tell yourself that you are worth it. That *you* are worthy.

Travel can push your limits in wonderful ways, contributing to longevity, because travel exercises body, brain, and mind.

As for the body, to travel easily, you need physical strength. Your back, legs, and arms are called into action when you handle your luggage (tip: pack lightly). Your feet and legs get a workout when you walk to see long-awaited sights. I clocked an impressive 24,877 steps one day on Prague's cobblestone streets. That was a challenge. The cobblestones are uneven. When you immerse yourself in a new culture, your stomach fills with new foods, like crickets in a food market in Beijing, fermented shark in Iceland, very bony Guinea pig in Peru, or rattlesnakes in Texas. On a trip to Japan, I thought I couldn't make it without coffee in the morning. But what a surprise it was to find out that my body was fine with their green tea. By a small stream in Kyoto, I had the best noodle dish ever, with kimchi, ginger, tofu, and a load of secret yummy ingredients. When you travel, *you find the deep muscle of the world,* says Mary Oliver.

I did something that I never expected I would do. I surprised myself. Enjoying the view of the majestic Pont Du Gard, the three-story aqueduct, built by the Romans in the year 50 AD, from the bank of the clear, clean, crystalline Gardon River in Southern France, I just stood there. My kids sensed my hesitation. They didn't accept *no.* So, I played along. I waded into the water, steadied myself in the river, let fish nibble at my legs, and then, I swam across to the other side, got out, sniffed the gorgeous yellow flowers, and swam back. Oh, the delight.

As for the brain, a certain thinking kicks in when planning a trip. Necessarily, you minimize the number of items you need. You put extra effort into remembering where things are. You practice resilience and find ways to calm yourself when dealing with things like no ATM, a misplaced charger, double-booked lodging, lost luggage, and the weather. Solving problems can become a game. You learn about different lifestyles like siestas in Mexico, midnight dinners in Spain, and closed shops on Sundays in many European countries. Your flexibility muscles get exercised when you travel. You may have to change plans, as we did, when a blizzard closed I-70 and we felt fortunate to spend the night on the floor in the only Limon, Colorado, truck stop.

As for the mind, when outside of our daily comfort zone, we can witness cultural belief systems other than our own. What a stimulation! On a group tour in Hong Kong, we visited a shrine nestled amongst skyscrapers. They say every wish comes true upon request at the Wong Tai Sin Temple, the home of three religions: Taoism, Buddhism, and Confucianism. Imagine! Harmony among religions? No missionary zeal? None of the my-God-is-better-than-your-God thing? Considering European ecclesiastic history, the crusades and such, that blew my mind. What an ingenious concept for religions to get along in one space. Progress for humankind! And that's not all. The temple presented a fourth option. Along its back wall, an array of booths housed soothsayers, palm readers, and astrologers. After a worshipper would kneel at one of the shrine's altars, they would make a wish, shake a bamboo cylinder with fortune sticks until one fell out, and exchange it for a piece of paper with the same number. That would be shown to the astrologer who told the fortune. It's good to know Mandarin or Cantonese if you visit.

A big trip every year is a great idea. And big is however you define it. It could be a day trip into the countryside beyond your city limits. Just an hour's drive from Kansas City, a whole new world opens up: the Flint Hills. A sea of grass. It's tallgrass and prairie to the horizon. Restoration of the tallgrass ecosystem happens here on abandoned farmland reversing environmental damage. Native seeds and seedlings of grasses and wildflowers are thriving—prairie violets, wavy-leaf thistles, white Western yarrow, yellow buffalo gourd, purple coneflowers, and more. This grassland is also home to a diversity of birds, insects, reptiles, and mammals. You can take a prairie tour.

If possible, I prefer to travel in the company of loved ones, and I don't hesitate to ask for assistance with transportation. Help is nearly always available. It sometimes gets you to the front of the line.

During my travels, I savor each moment. Travel instills gratitude for my own place. Oh, the memories I get to cherish when I'm back home. The meals, the awesome sights, the delightful purchases. I always bring back a special stone that tells a story of each place I visit.

Experiment with TRAVEL:

Where would you like to go?

Down the road or around the world?

Consider group travel with like-minded folks.

Take a journey in your armchair; mental travel, too, stimulates the imagination.

CHAPTER 21

U for UPDATE

Going With the Times and Even Forward

"Change is never easy, but always possible."
~ Barack Obama ~

F reshness contributes to well-being. It's good to feel new and relevant and not old-fashioned or outdated. So, get with it! Change is the fundamental way of the universe. Update!

Try an original look. New shoes, a sporty hoody, or an in-vogue headband. That hot pink jacket. How about a new haircut? A different color?

When I decided to update my gardening skills, I enrolled in an online University Extension Master Gardener Class. It required studying a 225-page core manual with thirty-two pages on insects alone, attending four months of Zoom classes, active participation in discussion boards, debating weekly questions in writing, and tests every Friday, all of this online. I had never taken a class online and thought it was a good thing for me to do during the isolation of Covid, but then I freaked out.

I made appointments with the local electronic store's computer help squad for browser consultations. I got frazzled over crashes, rebooting, and virus attacks. Access to the course material was occasionally denied. I tried to blame the computer, but I really had pressed the wrong button. I had to learn to Zoom: muted or unmuted, with or without video. I panicked over those darn intermittent internet outages, about being late on tests, and not participating enough in those chat rooms. But hey! I summoned my strength. I updated my computer hardware. I knew I could handle technology if only I persisted. Resilience kicked in and I began to feel a bit like a *badass*. I updated myself with a new attitude. That brought self-empowerment.

My favorite card game used to be Bridge. Wouldn't you know, Bridge rules have changed since the 1980s? Now I'm looking for a Bridge class to freshen up.

This one was a blow to my gut. Having lived in the US for decades, I decided to write letters about my American experience to my German relatives for Christmas; nice essays in English. Then I translated them into German, delighting in the fun of feeling the coziness of my mother tongue (even though at times I consulted a dictionary). I had the stories bound into little books. What I got back from my relatives was giggles about my German. Funny. Outdated. Weird. *So geht's ja nun nicht!* It doesn't work like that. Language, wouldn't you know, needs updating, too.

Update yourself on the news. Check in with your local radio stations on the air and online. Read the daily paper. Keep up with local, national, and international events.

Viewpoints need refreshing, too; how you look at things, how you weigh pros and cons, and how you judge. Our outlook on life makes or breaks our well-being. When I lived in Lexington, Kentucky, I shared a garden fence with Tom, my then eighty-year-old neighbor. He often ended a conversation with his mantra. "B and G," he said, smiling. "Bad and good." That was his wisdom. He invited me, the young thing, with his insights to update my immigrant thinking. After all, this was the South! Balance it out. There are two sides on any coin.

Bad and good on a global note: during the cold war, a line ran through Europe from North to South, severing the West from the Soviet bloc. This horrible death strip was called the Iron Curtain. In December 1989, the Berlin Wall fell, and with it the Iron Curtain. In that strip, German conservationists created a wildlife corridor from Finland to Greece. It is now a flourishing habitat and a protected migration path for over 600 species of birds and mammals.

On a personal note, the death of my husband of fifty-five years was terrible. After a while, for my own sake, I changed my way of thinking about it. I saw it as a fresh start, which any ending can instill. For the first time in a long while, I focused on what *I* wanted to do.

Updating is one thing. Being progressive is even better. Think about installing solar panels on your roof, a sauna in your basement, or a rainwater collection system for your garden. Think about changing the way you purchase food. Instead of relying on mass-produced groceries, know where your food comes from. Check out the resources in your countryside. We contracted with a small local farm, Moxie Farm north of Kansas City, Missouri, to provide us with seasonal organic vegetables, organic eggs, butter, bone broth, and meat from their farm-raised happy animals. We pick up our order weekly. There's a bit of time involved, but we support sustainable organic farming, which is best for the environment and best for our gut health.

UPDATE suggestions:

Invest in a new set of kitchen towels.
A new doormat.
Change your smoke alarm batteries.
Refresh your wardrobe; buy one thing and throw out two.
Think of future projects.

CHAPTER 22

V for VOLUNTEERING

Sharing Your Bliss

*"Good actions give strength to ourselves and
inspire good actions in others."*

~ Plato ~

In the Sanjusangen-do Temple in Kyoto, Japan, built in 1164 AD, 1,000 human-sized golden statues surround Kannon, the Buddhist Goddess of Compassion. Each statue extends her forty-two arms and hands, offering gifts to the world.

Volunteering is the super energy that gets us off the couch. It gives us a reason to be.

According to Aristotle, the ancient Greek philosopher, the essence of life (drumroll, please) is, *to serve others and do good.* Volunteering lifts the mood, encourages better self-care, and decreases stress. Service to others increases positive and relaxed feelings by releasing dopamine in the brain. Volunteering makes us feel socially connected; it wards off loneliness. If you are looking for meaning, self-empowerment, and appreciation, volunteering could be the thing for you.

Volunteering is associated with a lower risk of dying. Volunteers just live longer.

One of my favorite ways to volunteer is also my favorite way to socialize. I party with a purpose. I run a local chapter of the nonprofit organization Together Women Rise (TWR), formerly called Dining for Women. The members of TWR help fund health, education, and business venture programs worldwide to benefit women and girls. No religion, state, or men are involved in the process. (Apologies to my gentlemen readers.) Every month highlights a different program.

The way it works is easy. I, like all chapter leaders in the US and around the world, host potluck dinners at home. I ask my friends to bring a dish to share and a cash donation of whatever amount, large or small, in the amount they would spend if they had gone out to eat. We watch a video of the issue of the month and discuss it over our potluck dinners. Women support women all over the world. The projects that most inspired me over the years were smoke free cooking stoves for Guatemala. Without them, the women inhale the smoke together with their babies strapped on their backs. Birthing kits for women in the Amazon were another of my favorites, along with leadership programs teaching girls and young women coping and negotiation skills in occupied Palestine. At the end of each evening together, my friends ask, "When's the next one?"

As a family, we volunteered at Heart to Heart International. We assembled hygiene kits for disaster areas that each included: a toothbrush, toothpaste, a comb, soap, a washcloth, a small towel, and nail clippers, all in a sturdy, reusable plastic see-through bag. We wondered who would open the bags, who would touch these objects next, what the people went through, and what their personal challenges were. This was a perfect teaching experience for my granddaughter. Considering the disasters currently in the world, when the situation seems hopeless, when we feel we cannot help, this is a way to actually do something.

There are many ways to volunteer. Experience is our asset. As elders, we all have wisdom to share. We have knowledge, expertise, skills, and more free time than we ever had. Our compassion and empathy have grown because we know what it is like to deal with change chosen and change forced. Send good vibes. Teach kids how to read through your local library. How about joining the effort to deliver meals to persons who are shut in and live alone through Meals on Wheels America? You may require this service yourself someday. Caring for foster dogs and cats through a local animal shelter by taking them into your home for a period of time is a need you could meet. Ushering at a theatre or opera house can be fun, and you get to see the performance for free. Collecting litter on your walk is a small thing but has a big impact when everyone does it.

I joined the annual Missouri River cleanup sponsored by the Missouri River Relief Program. In rubber boots, with heavy-duty gloves, a sturdy blue trash bag, and a grabber, I spent a most delightful Saturday morning in the company of 200 younger volunteers on the banks of the Missouri River. That river, the longest in the US, became my river for the day. In one morning of volunteering, I exercised several ideas from this book, such as:

* **Believing** that I, as an individual, can make a difference

* **Forgiveness** for the polluters

* **Independence** in choosing how to spend that morning

❋   **Joy** as I was filling that blue bag, and then a second one

❋   **Knowing** this was important

❋   **Moving** along the river's edge, bending, squatting, stretching, and using new muscles

❋   **Nature** by being outdoors close to water on a beautiful day

❋   **Purpose** by actively making the world a better place

❋   **Socializing** with new people

❋   **Yes** —I had the determination to do some good

Don't ever resist a giving impulse, just go for it. Practice generosity. You can't take it with you, they say. Donate to your favorite cause, the arts, the environment, the world.

VOLUNTEERING:

What skills do you have to offer?

Contribute to your neighborhood, to your community.

Learn more about Together Women Rise at togetherwomenrise.org. Maybe you can start a chapter or join one in your area.

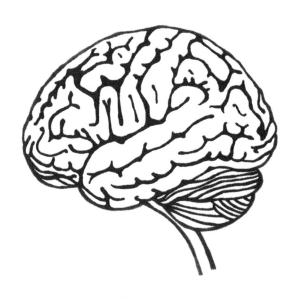

CHAPTER 23

W for WONDER

Brain Enrichment, Brain Exercise, Brain Food

"Curiosity is the lust of the mind."
~ Thomas Hobbes ~

The verb *to wonder* means *being curious*. When we ask: Why? When? How? Wondering is the key to growth on all levels.

As a kid, you probably used to wonder a lot. Now, cultivate that unrelenting curiosity with the same vigor as your three-year-old self. That kind of unbridled curiosity strengthens the brain, creating new neural pathways and improving your brain's infrastructure. Yep, a very good thing.

How do you improve your brain? By thinking new thoughts. By solving problems. And by challenging it to have fun in fresh and exciting ways. Ask questions you never asked before, such as:

❋   Why are daisy petals arranged the way they are?

❋   Can I compost with no fuss?

❋   How does a solar roof work? Would it work for me?

❋   Do harmonies play in outer space?

❋   How did the first seed appear on Earth? The first flower?

❋   How can flocks of birds and schools of fish move in synchrony?

❋   Can I learn to sing an aria?

Wondering doesn't have to be complicated. Curiosity and creativity hold hands as best friends and lovers. They walk together.

Be curious about food and act upon it. Try out noodles with feta and tomatoes or crustless spinach quiche. Experiment with wines. The world has enjoyed them ever since the Greek god Dionysus raised the first goblet on Mount Olympus.

Be curious about art: gallery showings, live concerts, museum talks, storytelling events. You can explore virtual museum tours online. Try a new theatre, even the opera. Lots of fun.

Curiosity can start just outside your door. There are probably places in your town tourists come to see and they are new to you, too. Try a new restaurant. Visit a farmers' market in a different part of the city. Explore a new park. Be curious about community gatherings and local issues at your city hall. Discover treasures through your public library—you pay the taxes to finance it. It's okay to open books in the middle and see if they grab you. If not, just try another one.

Be curious about the world. Stay informed about current affairs. Get your news from more than one source. Keep alive your ability to debate about present day issues with trusted friends who respect your opinions. Cultivate a safe zone debate partner. Be curious about other cultures. Learn a new language: French, Navajo, Kernowek.

Be curious about people. Ask questions. Prompt them to talk about themselves and listen to them deeply. Everyone has an interesting story to tell.

Best of all, be curious about yourself. Ask what else you might try in this lifetime. The major life decisions more than likely have already been made. Now, what else? Surprise yourself with what you can come up with. How about a new sport? My oldest son wanted me to try pickleball. I did horseback riding instead—they have step stools at the stable for easy ascent. After that experience, I didn't walk right for a few days. Next time I will request a less-wide horse.

And then there is *to wonder* meaning as being *in awe*. In awe about the universe, about nature, about trust, and about love.

Seek WONDER in your life:

Give yourself permission to be curious.

List three things you want to know.

Find out the last vote of the official who represents you in your state.

Learn counting to ten in a foreign language.

Gaze at the Milky Way.

CHAPTER 24

X for EXTRA

Truly Extraordinary

*"Always remember that you are absolutely
unique. Just like everyone else."*
~ Margaret Mead ~

The many roles we played in our lives, the goals we achieved, the successes we had, and the mistakes we learned from have made us who we are. Let's embrace it all! Each of us is unique. You are unique. I'm unique. Let's engage in positive self-talk and keep that going; and admire and respect ourselves with kindness.

It's an enigma that you, that I, that we all are here. We survived childhood, came through adolescence, made the decisions of early adulthood, managed the middle age crisis, and arrived at this point in life, the senior years. Alleluia.

Let us consider the immensity of the universe and the time it took for humans to evolve. Our presence on Earth is unique, regardless of age. But being an elder is mind-boggling. I see it as a sign of amazing grace. If our very existence is not magic, I don't know what is.

Join me in this exercise:

My favorite activity is ...

My dream is ...

My favorite dish is ...

My favorite flower is ...

My favorite music is ...

My favorite poet is ...

This is my motto ...

CHAPTER 25

Y for YES

It Opens New Doors

*"Once you make a decision, the universe
conspires to make it happen."*
~ Ralph Waldo Emerson ~

I almost made the letter Y about Youthfulness. Then I realized that, truly, my book is about the opposite. It's about acknowledging our very age, about embracing what we have experienced, what we know, and what we have become. Yes, accepting that with gusto. Call it elderliness. Call it earned wisdom. Call it vibrant maturity. This phase of life is not about being bored, or being dull or faded, which can happen at any age. It's about being animated, energetic, and upbeat, having lust for life, wanting to do things, and engaging with the world with vigor. Make sure your current year can be your best.

So, rally your stamina. Cultivate your will. In Latin, *will* (*voluntas)* means choice, intention, mental strength, resolve. In old English, *will* means delight, desire, determination, joy, mind, pleasure, request, wish. All of that. Garner that will! Say, *Yes!* Address that leaky spot in the ceiling, finish that project, make that doctor's appointment, be optimistic. Tell yourself *yes, I can!* Once convinced that you are doing what is right, you have the will to act and not quit. Will leads to decisions.

Say yes to:

* ❈ Adventures
* ❈ Balance of activity and rest
* ❈ Being with people, young and old
* ❈ Decorating with a seasonal touch
* ❈ Dressing up for Halloween
* ❈ Eating outside
* ❈ Enjoying life
* ❈ Experimenting with the activities in this book
* ❈ Fresh veggies, homemade food, and dark chocolate
* ❈ Hanging clothes outside to dry
* ❈ Hugging
* ❈ Inspiring people
* ❈ Laughing your head off
* ❈ Loving yourself
* ❈ Loving others—Picasso said, "there is no love, only acts of love."
* ❈ One thing at a time
* ❈ Opposing common opinions, like the rebel you can be sometimes
* ❈ Owning your decisions

❋   Playing new games on game nights

❋   Recycling, repurposing, and reusing

❋   Seeking the unusual

❋   Singing

❋   Standing tall

You've got the power to say yes.

YES! You may like to:

Do one new thing today.

Speak with someone you don't know.

Walk an unmarked trail in the park.

CHAPTER 26

Z for ZEN

The Other Side of the Grass

*"If you don't know how to die, don't worry. Nature will
tell you what to do on the spot, fully and adequately."*
~ Michel de Montaigne ~

I live in the woods. It's a wild place where I can forest bathe. And there is wildlife. Over the years, I have clapped, gesticulated, and shouted at woodpeckers who hammer on my house. Maybe they were attracting a mate. Maybe they were excavating a nest hole. Maybe they were feeding on insects in my siding, or stashing away acorns, or marking their territory. "Get away! Stay in the woods, guys!" I shouted. They would flit up into the nearest tree and watch me acting out, rolling their eyes and shrugging their feathery shoulders.

One morning, I opened my front door, and on my sunny stoop lay a magnificent woodpecker—bright red cap and crown, black and white zebra striped plumage, pale belly, and open eyes. Dead. I stood with it for a while. The universe was telling me to remember death in life. "You are beautiful," I said to the bird. "I'm sorry I raised my voice."

I wrapped him in a paper towel and buried him under my honeysuckle bush. Since that day, I have placed foot-high owl statues around my bushes and hammered metal woodpecker impersonators on my house walls, indicating to my feathery friends that my house is being watched and that the territory has been taken.

When my husband, the doctor, scientist, and teacher, had a heart attack, the ER nurse heard his accent and asked where he was from. He wanted her to guess. "European, maybe Polish?" she suggested.

He turned his head to the wall and was gone. Instantly. Just like the bird who fell from flight. It was a Sunday in May. My husband had seen patients in our office the day before. That night is etched in my memory with its panic, sadness, and resolve. We all know how swiftly life can change completely, and how precious life is. Call the kids. Call the relatives.

The day before the funeral, I went farther than usual on my morning walk. Way down to the lake, onto the dam between the valley on the left and the water on the right. It was a very calm day. Not one leaf shook. When crossing the dam, suddenly I could feel it: a burst of air embraced my neck from behind with a warm, gentle intensity. Like the touch of a fur stole. I sensed exuberant joy wrapped into a caress. I knew it was him. No question. He was telling me that he was alright, but that he couldn't stay. I returned home and went into my garden. My purple irises were in bloom, abundant, lush, and aromatic like never before. I cut a bouquet, severing the stems from their rhizomes close to the ground. They would be back next spring. We laid them on his coffin. His end was not *the* end. He had let me know it was a new beginning for him and me.

An American ash tree, taller than eighty feet, older than eighty years, glorious in its bright golden yellow fall colors, thrived in front of my window. Death came to it by an invasion of emerald ash borers. It had to be cut down. I miss its majesty and presence. But also, now, I can see more sky and the wildflowers get the sun they so desire.

Acknowledge grief, panic, and sadness, but let them pass through without trying to hold them. There is peace waiting for you; calmness, love, and wisdom that can bring you to your knees.

ZEN for your consideration:

Have things death-ready.

Make or revisit your will.

Let your wishes be known.

Have a power of attorney document.

How would you like to die?

Raise a glass.
Here's to you.
Here's to us.
May we celebrate.

Fun Reads

Attia, Peter with Bill Gifford. *Outlive. The Science & Art of Longevity*. Harmony Books, New York, 2023.

Aurelius, Marcus. *Meditations. A New Translation with an Introduction by Gregory Hays*. The Modern Library, New York, 2002.

Buettner, Dan. *Blue Zone Secrets for Living Longer*. National Geographic Society, Washington, D.C., 2023.

Buettner, Dan. *The Blue Zones American Kitchen. 100 Recipes to Live to 100*. National Geographic Society, Washington, D.C., 2022.

Byrne, Lorna. *Angels in My Hair*. Century Random House, London, 2008.

Epictetus: *The Art of Living. The Classic Manual on Virtue, Happiness, and Effectiveness. A New Interpretation by Sharon Lebell*. Harper Collins Publishers, New York, NY, 1995.

Friedman, David. *Food Sanity. How to Eat in a World of Fads and Fiction*. Basic Health Publications, Turner Publishing Company. Nashville, TN, New York, NY, 2018.

Gigliotti, Carol. *The Creative Lives of Animals*. New York University Press, New York, 2022.

Gilbert, Elizabeth. *Big Magic. Creative Living Beyond Fear*. Riverhead Books, New York, 2015.

Haupt, Lyanda L. *Rooted. Life at the Crossroads of Science, Nature, and Spirit*. Little, Brown Spark, New York, 2021.

Kimmerer, Robin Wall. *Braiding Sweetgrass. Indigenous Wisdom, Scientific Knowledge, and the Teachings of Plants*. Milkweed Editions, Canada, 2013.

Kondo, Marie. *The Life-Changing Magic of Tidying Up. The Japanese Art of Decluttering and Organizing*. Ten Speed Press, Berkeley, CA, 2011.

Ober, Clinton et al. *Earthing. The Most Important Health Discovery Ever!* Basic Health Publications, Inc., Laguna Beach, CA, 2014.

Sacred Places of a Lifetime. 500 of the World's Most Peaceful and Powerful Destinations. Introduced by Keith Bellows. National Geographic, Toucan Books Ltd., Washington, D.C., 2008.

Stillman, Scott. *Nature's Silent Message*. Wild Soul Press, Boulder, CO, 2020.

Wohlleben, Peter. *The Hidden Life of Trees. What They Feel, How They Communicate. Discoveries from a Secret World*. Ludwig Verlag München, 2015.

Acknowledgments

I am so incredibly grateful for:

My daughter Julia Othmer, editor and illustrator, for her unwavering commitment to authenticity and truth.

My sons, Konstantin and Philipp Othmer, for cheering me on.

Patricia Hamarstrom Williams for her laughter, her sense of drama, and her sharp pen.

Mary Linda Hughes for her gentle, strong focus on humanity.

Keith Chrostovski, for always listening to me on our dog walks.

Dorrit Bender for her common-sense kindness after reading the (very) first draft.

James Lundie for his calm confidence that I would be finding the right title.

Mary Lou Reid for her enthusiasm in coaching me.

Geoffrey Berwind, boss, for showing me the ropes on subtitles.

Dr. David Friedman for being so magnificent and amazingly prompt.

The production team at the Steve Harrison Group for their Monday night coaching call assurance.

Cristina Smith for organizing everything.

Valerie Costa for her humor and her patience.

Christy Day for her exquisite sense of design and color.

Cynthia Janzen for help with the audio book.

Silver Wainhouse in Uzès, France, for her flair and for getting my vibe.

The City of Parkville, Missouri, for keeping my town peaceful.

My neighbors for inspiring me.

Thank you all. I could not have done it without you.

Credits and Permissions

The short quotations used in this book are considered to be fair use. They were obtained through internet searches. The websites did not charge for the quotes or indicate whether the quotations were subject to copyright protection.

James T. Lundie gave permission to quote lyrics and play the theme song "For the Trees" on my website.

About the Author

Sieglinde Othmer, PhD earned her doctorate in social sciences at the University of Hamburg, Germany. A refugee, immigrant, academic, administrator, researcher, and gardener, she raised three children and three dogs, and has traveled to over forty countries. In this book, she shares the wisdom she has acquired in eighty years of living. She is a board member of the United Nations Greater Kansas City chapter. She resides in Parkville, Missouri, on a lake where Canada geese fly over, where blue herons fish, and where great horned owls keep night watch. Her purpose is to help people feel good about their age. At any age.

Website: www. joyouslongevity.com
email: joyouslongevity@gmail.com